Praise for *Trusting God Through Testing Times*

In her book, *Trusting God Through Testing Times,* Jill draws from deep wells of imbedded scripture and personal experience. Through insight and practical application, she encourages you hold firmly to the faith and peace found in the Word, not allowing yourself to become double-minded and fearful when the world shakes under your feet.

Having faced her own share of trials with grace and the strength that only God can give, this book feels as if Jill brings you into her living room, sits across the coffee table from you and shares her heart. This is a must have for anyone who has had their life interrupted by the unexpected personal explosion, for upon these pages she points you toward a balm that will heal all wounds.

~Barbie Loflin, Assistant Pastor
Springhouse Worship & Arts Center

In Jill Grossman's book, *Trusting God Through Testing Times,* she guides us by explaining the scriptures that build trust in the promises and character of God. Everyone lives through times of testing and needs the signs along the way to find a place of rest. She goes on to show that we require the divine perspective to continue to live by faith.

Jill's theme is hope, as she explains verses that pertain to common problems. "Wisdom is seeing ourselves in any situation and applying God's truth accordingly." Be prepared to discover practical steps toward finding hope in the midst of testing times.

~Bruce Coble, Missions Pastor
Springhouse Worship and Arts Center

When Jill asked me to review her book, I took it seriously. After reading this work of art, I am seriously convinced this is a good word to the body of Christ. Love the amount of scripture used to back up the lessons and I love how Jill is transparent with her own struggles. The four books—James, Job, and 1 & 2 Thessalonians—prepare us to live out our own Christian life through trials, struggles, and circumstances.

And, I love the challenge at the end—if you are not a Believer—"Are you ready to make the most important decision in your life?" I recommend this book to all Believers – mature, marginal, or just plain messed up.

~Derek Faulkner, Executive Director,
Renewed Life Ministries Outreach

Jill Grossman has given us practical examples and illustrations of how to walk through the testing times in our lives in accordance with the Word of God. A great companion to God's words to us in James, Job, and 1 & 2 Thessalonians.

~Sallie Courtoy, Area Director
Community Bible Study

TRUSTING GOD THROUGH TESTING TIMES

Trusting God Through Testing Times

A Journey Through James, Job and the Thessalonians

Jill Grossman

WordCrafts

Trusting God Through Testing Times
A Journey Through James, Job and the Thessalonians
Copyright © 2017
Jill Grossman

Cover design and author photo by David Warren

All rights reserved. No part of this book may be reproduced, stored in a retrieval system, or transmitted in any form or by any means – electronic, mechanical, photocopy, recording, or otherwise – without the prior written permission of the publisher. The only exception is brief quotations for review purposes.

Unless otherwise noted all Scripture quotations are taken from THE HOLY BIBLE, NEW INTERNATIONAL VERSION®, NIV® Copyright © 1973, 1978, 1984, 2011 by Biblica, Inc.™ Used by permission. All rights reserved worldwide.

Scripture quotations marked (MSG) taken from THE MESSAGE. Copyright © by Eugene H. Peterson 1993, 1994, 1995, 1996, 2000, 2001, 2002. Used by permission of NavPress. All rights reserved. Represented by Tyndale House Publishers, Inc.

Scripture quotations marked (AMP) taken from the Amplified® Bible, Copyright © 1954, 1958, 1962, 1964, 1965, 1987 by The Lockman Foundation Used by permission. (www.Lockman.org)

Scripture quotations marked (NASB) taken from the New American Standard Bible®, Copyright © 1960, 1962, 1963, 1968, 1971, 1972, 1973, 1975, 1977, 1995 by The Lockman Foundation. Used by permission. (www.Lockman.org)

Scripture quotations marked (HCSB) are taken from the Holman Christian Standard Bible®, Used by Permission HCSB ©1999,2000,2002,2003,2009 Holman Bible Publishers. Holman Christian Standard Bible®, Holman CSB®, and HCSB® are federally registered trademarks of Holman Bible Publishers.

Scripture quotations marked (ESV) are from the ESV® Bible (The Holy Bible, English Standard Version®), copyright © 2001 by Crossway, a publishing ministry of Good News Publishers. Used by permission. All rights reserved.

Published by WordCrafts Press
Buffalo, WY 82834
www.wordcrafts.net

CONTENTS

Foreword   i
Preface   iii

The Book of James   1

James' Challenges   2
Our Faith and Our Trials   6
Playing Favorites   19
There's Power in the Tongue   27
Finding Humility   38
Attitude Adjustments   46

The Book of Job   57

Job's Challenges   58
The Tests and Trials of Job   65
Accusations and Bad Advice   74
Wisdom Comes in All Ages   86
When God Speaks…   98
God Forgives and God Restores   108

The Books of 1 & 2 Thessalonians   119

Paul's Challenge   120
Following Paul's Model of Faith   126
Persecutions and Pressures   136
Living a Life of Readiness   152
Justice, Encouragement and Warning   160
Standing in Truth   174

Epilogue   186
In Conclusion   189
Study Questions   194
Acknowledgements   212
About the Author   213

FOREWORD

Being a fan and advocate of Jill's first book, *A Revelation of Love*, I was eager to provide a foreword for this book. I present my thoughts on this inspiring, informative and needed book with the deepest respects that are heartfelt and with great admiration!

Where do our stories come from? Are you a growing a repository of spiritual stories? How's that working—or not? How are your testimonies (Rev. 12:1)?

Many wonder why we do not enjoy a prevailing and abundant Christianity. It is because we aren't growing our own faith story. Well, help has arrived! Again and again my friend, Jill Grossman, seasons the struggles we face with selected scriptures, illustrations and pithy take-a—ways to make it more appealing to own our adversities and grow our stories.

If you'd like to learn how to take the grit of life and "handle it like an oyster" until it becomes a cherished pearl in your character, this is the book. Jill has composed a true companion to the conflicts and crises of our lives. Through the grease-cutting counsel of James, the influences exacted upon Job, and the example of Paul in the Thessalonian letters, she gives the reader an abundance of take-a-ways for *Trusting God Through Testing Times*.

We then realize that perhaps we haven't viewed adversities correctly—as opportunities for the development of our eternal nature. We have misconstrued the tough times and missed the stories God wants to grow within us. When stuff happens, we have easily defaulted from spiritual confidence in Christ to a humanistic mentality of "why is this happening to me?"

Jill reminds us that we must wrap our minds around it and deal with this as quickly as possible. We must personally develop a disciplined response to trust Him and not our understanding of things, as stated in Proverbs 3:5-6. We learn that it is the accumulation of our life experiences, accompanied by faith that qualifies us to empathize, encourage and rescue others. As this grows within us we can envision every adversity as an opportunity for making Christ manifest to others who watch our responses, just as onlookers long ago watched Paul, the Apostle.

The time has come for you and me to accept the process of God's Word that promises, "many are the afflictions of the righteous but the Lord will deliver you through them all."

So then, you are now about to open Jill's carefully assembled "toolbox for trials" which will be an incredibly wise resource for your construction toward a greater destiny—as Christ has intended for you all along. So, taking this book in one hand and the Bible in the other, you'll make the most of every adversity you encounter, and "come forth as gold" through tough times. God's favor will indeed be yours as you apply the truth, wisdom and guidance afforded through this study companion.

Randy Berg, Friend and Pastor of
Grace Church
LaVergne, Tennessee

PREFACE

Over the past several years, I've often been within earshot when people say things like, "I wish God would stop putting me through this!" or "This is a test, I just know it!" or "God must hate me!"

Life can have its challenges for sure. My husband, Steve, and I can certainly attest to testing times that we have been through. We've had so many over the years.

For example: Many years ago as we were starting our family my dad was diagnosed with a terminal disease called ALS (Amyotrophic Lateral Sclerosis), or better known as Lou Gehrig's Disease. The diagnosis was grim and he had about 3 years or so to live. ALS is a debilitating disease so as time progressed, so would his disease. Right in the middle of all of this my mom was diagnosed with Kidney Cancer and had six months to live!

At the time my mom got sick my dad was already wheelchair bound from his disease. My mother's cancer revealed itself through a stroke and left her wheelchair bound as well. So now we had two parents in wheelchairs. To add complication to the situation my sister, brother, and I all lived far away from my parents who lived in Texas. My sister lived several hours away, my brother was in Wisconsin, and I was in Tennessee. Both my sister and my brother had executive jobs and we had just had a baby. This was a huge crisis!

But God gives grace as we go through trials and grows us into a deeper relationship with Him.

My husband was on the road during a lot of this time, but this helped increase our income. It gave us the stability that allowed me to go back to

Texas for extended time periods with our baby in tow and oversee things at my parent's house. My brother came in every other month or so to oversee the business side of things. He worked at his job as best as he could from their house. This was before computers and cell phones so he was on the house phone constantly. My sister would come in every weekend or two and work on Medicare and insurance issues for them. We had to hire home health care workers and nurses too.

Everything changed and shifted in our lives from that point. I was trying to raise a baby and hold on to my marriage during all of this, too. Soon, my mom did pass away and my dad passed away a year and 3 months later. But not before he ended up marrying his care taker six weeks before he died...another crisis! (That story is for another time).

But during those three and a half years of enormous trials, there were blessings, too. There are always blessings to find in the midst of the storms. Our parents got to see what their children were truly made of. As siblings, we saw each other in a new light and recognized and respected the strengths we had. And Steve and I learned what strength in marriage was. Sometimes a crisis has a way of bonding you. God's Word became more real to me than I had ever experienced before. I also began to see what true friendship means and who sticks closer to you like a brother—and who doesn't.

I remember being at a party and someone wanted Steve to explain what we had just gone through with my folks. When he finished, a friend said, "Oh, I could never go through that!" Steve politely answered, "You haven't been asked to, yet."

Nothing escapes God's watch. I don't believe we were being punished or God caused this crisis to teach us as a lesson. But He did give us the grace to walk through it. If we are asked to go through something we need to know—and more importantly to trust- that God will bring us through it, and we will be more the wiser for it. Trusting takes faith, right? Sometimes it takes really great faith. But remember, we walk "*through* the valley of the shadow of death ..." we don't stay there (Psalm 23). Maybe God has been preparing us for something big that's around the corner! We may not know how, but we do know that the way out is to trust in the promises of God and to trust in the character of God. We need a boot camp of sorts to help prepare us.

I don't know what challenges you are going through, but there is hope.

And that hope is in God's Word! What better way to get answers to where we are in life than through the Word of God?

We all can give advice, even great advice, but if we don't understand God's Word and learn to apply it to our lives first, the advice ends up just being noise. We need the foundation of God's Word to build and grow from first, and then the rest will fall into place.

As the World Changes

Many believe that we have entered a new season here on earth. Times are changing and things are heating up in the world. There's a spirit of division and a spirit of humanism that is prevalent. There is more greed and selfishness in people than we've noticed before and there is a spirit of entitlement that is present. It seems clear we are moving toward end time prophecies as the world begins to deteriorate. We just don't know God's time table and He does not work in our understanding of time.

But just like the parable of the ten virgins who were waiting for the bridegroom with their lamps and oil (Matthew 25), we must be ready too! And part of getting ready is to study His Word. We must *not* be foolish, like the five of the virgins were in the parable, but wise and prepared as we wait like the other five virgins who were. They were rewarded for their obedience because only they were able to enter the wedding banquet with the bridegroom when He appeared.

Are We Ready?

I kept asking myself, *are* we ready? Are we mature enough, prepared enough to go through testing times as our world becomes spiritually darker? Do we know how to be obedient as we wait? Do we know how to walk through a crisis and not blame God for it?

That is why I first chose to teach, and now write, about these particular books of the Bible. I thought, if we must go through trials and tests in life, then let's study together and let the Holy Spirit be our advisor, counselor, and teacher along the way.

As I dug into James, Job, and 1 & 2 Thessalonians, I found many cross references that powerfully show us the wisdom and truth that is coming from both Old and New Testament teachings. What better foundation can be laid to help us mature and endure in our trials than with the truth of scripture? *How* does God and *what* does God want us to learn here? These books form a perfect study for us full of what we need for trials and tests that come our way.

Here's a summary of what I found:

1. The book of James gives us practical advice and lays out a foundation for us to mature by.
2. The book of Job gives us an almost unbelievable example to show us God's sovereignty and that we don't have to have complete understanding either.
3. The two books of Thessalonians help us put all of this into action-steps for when we are being pursued and persecuted— and persecuted can mean even by believers, too.

It's all about answering the question: How do we overcome? When life tests us, how do we make it work for us and not against us? We gain wisdom from God's Word and that results in a Christian who is maturing in his/her walk with Christ and that can help others mature in their walk as well. It's like that child's game, *A Barrel of Monkeys*. The idea is to hook as many monkeys together as you can and pull them up and out of the barrel. As we grow, we reach up to others who have gone before us and we use the other hand to grab someone and help them up along the way. This is the Christian walk. It puts a fresh spin on the old saying, "Life's just a barrel of monkeys!"

The Best Way to Receive This Study

This is what I have found when doing any kind of study. You get out of it, what you put into it. With that said, at the top of each chapter, beneath the title, there are Bible chapter divisions to read first; then read the chapter in this book. Remember, this is a study *guide* to help deepen your understanding of what you're learning.

If you don't have time to read the Bible sections first, I understand, that's OK. You'll still be able to follow along and have it make sense. But my heart is to point you to the Bible so I want to encourage you to read the chapters when you can.

I try to give a little historical background to help with the setting and context of what is going on in the scriptures in the introductions of each book. This will help lay a better foundation for you.

My hope is this journey will deepen your understanding and help you to stand firm in the challenges you may be facing. He has not forgotten you and He won't drop you either. Look to the Lord and not to your own circumstances. Believe His Word and trust in His character.

My hope is you begin to feel God's loving heart for you and you also begin to hear your Shepherd's voice through these scriptures and gain strength for yourself as you journey through this study.

I have also included study questions at the end of this book. These can be used as you go through each chapter, after you have finished the book, and even in a group setting. They are provided as a way to help you get as much out of these three Bible books as you possibly can.

Remember, He's the same yesterday, today and tomorrow. His promises are true and you can trust in that. Now let's begin our journey through these powerful books.

THE BOOK OF JAMES
GROWING IN MATURITY

JAMES' CHALLENGES

The book of James is filled with some of the most practical teachings in the New Testament. This is one of the reason's it's such a popular book. James writes clearly and simply—and at times he is quite direct. We could use a little directness in this day and age!

Many Bible scholars believe James' focus for his audience was the Jewish followers of Christ. The book of James is considered to be one of the earliest New Testament writings, (with the exception of Galatians), which might explain his practical approach to the life of faith. That is the essence of Jewish theology—*practicality*.

Much of our abstract thinking in Western philosophy is the result of the Greeks and their influence that they had on the early church. There's a tendency to take that abstract philosophical approach to the life we live and the level of morality we live it by. This has influenced the practice of our faith in the western world.

The book of James provides an excellent balance for us as he urges us to seek a practical approach to living out our faith.

About James

Imagine being the half-brother to Jesus Christ! A person can react to such a thing in one of two ways—with envy, jealousy and inferiority, or with respect and admiration that leads to discipleship.

James, being human, probably did both. In John 7:5 it says, *"For even his own brothers did not believe in him."*

But James did become a believer and follower of Christ, and also became a respected leader of the early church.

He was writing to the Jews who had been seeking God for thousands of years. What's nice for the reader is that his letter is clear and forthright. It is like a blueprint for Christian living. James addresses how circumstances can affect mature Christians, Christian relationships, our speech, and our heart attitudes.

He looks at himself first. James could have called himself a leader, a pillar of the church, but instead he uses the term *doulos*, meaning; "servant." He was a *servant-leader*. There's a big difference in a leader and a servant-leader. Most of us tend to be like the disciples who were concerned about which of them was the greatest. Some leaders we know are just like that; their focus is on themselves and what they've achieved. A servant-leader is "others"-focused and Jesus was the perfect model for us to follow on that. Clearly, James had learned Christ's ways when he heard Christ say to His disciples,

> *"Instead, whoever wants to become great among you must be your servant, and whoever wants to be first must be your slave—just as the Son of Man did not come to be served, but to serve, and to give his life as a ransom for many."*
>
> Matthew 20:26-28

Rory Noland, who wrote *Foundations in a Music Ministry*, pointed out the differences between a "Volunteer" and a "Servant-Leader" that I have found to be helpful. Here are twelve points that will help you see the difference. Which one are you?

1. A volunteer looks upon ministry as another commitment that they're obligated to fulfill, but a servant looks upon service as an opportunity to be used by God.
2. A volunteer looks upon any constructive criticism with indignation, but a servant is grateful for feedback because they want to be the best they can be.
3. A volunteer puts in minimum effort, but a servant puts in maximum effort.

4. A volunteer sits back and complains about things, but a servant looks for ways to help.
5. A volunteer feels threatened by the talents of others, but a servant feels secure in God's direction in their life.
6. A volunteer does no additional study or preparation (after all, they're just volunteering), but a servant is committed to being as prepared as possible.
7. A volunteer wants to quit at the first sign of adversity or discouragement, but a servant digs in and perseveres, trusting in the Lord.
8. A volunteer is oblivious to the needs of those around them, but a servant is sensitive to others and prays for them.
9. A volunteer is more prone to jealousy of others, but a servant praises God for distributing gifts and talents as He chooses.
10. A volunteer shrinks back from resolving relational conflicts, but a servant seeks to resolve all relational conflicts to preserve the unity of the team with which they serve.
11. A volunteer's main source of fulfillment is her talents and abilities, but a servant knows that being used by God is the most fulfilling thing they can do with their life.
12. A volunteer can't handle being put into a situation where they are stretched, but a servant responds to God with a humble dependence on Him.

Jesus was secure in the Father, and James was secure in Jesus. James may have been Jesus' half-brother but he called Jesus "Lord" and "Master." It seems that James had one concern, and that was to please his Lord.

Do we live our lives with that in mind? Is this our one objective?

A servant may minister to his master directly, but he's equally serving when he carries out his master's concerns. That was James' ambition. He could have sought political gain for himself by writing to the Roman leaders or only writing to those Christian leaders with the popular reputations. Instead he demonstrated his love for the Jewish Christians who were scattered all around. If James could help those who were dispersed to become mature in Christ, God's glory would be spread among the nations in which they were all scattered.

> **Christian maturity enables us to be true servants.**

There's a story of a Chinese farmer who had left a Christian compound after having cataracts removed from his eyes. A few days later, the missionary doctor looked out his window and noticed this same man whose eyes had just been corrected—holding the end of a rope, a long rope. Holding on to that rope in single file, were several dozen blind Chinese men and women, whom he'd rounded up and led for miles to the doctor who had worked a "miracle" on his eyes.[1]

In the same way, James having his own eyes opened to understand true Christian life, sent his letter like a rope - a lifeline - to new, confused, and struggling Jewish Christians everywhere—that they too might come to the Great Physician for correction of their sight.

James was written specifically to the 1st century people but it has a universal appeal and application to all who read it. It is classified as one of the general epistles, which means it is not addressed to a particular church or person, but to a general audience.[2] It is a collection of useful instructions that we can use to help us walk out our faith.

There are many parallels between the attitude of the culture then and the one we live in now. Back then the Roman Empire had already hit its peak and was beginning its decline. The spirit of the age was one of cynicism and morality and ethics were at an all time low. Sound familiar? Solomon was right! He said there is, *"Nothing new under the sun* (Ecclesiastes 1:9)." We are declining.

Yet then and now, God calls us to the same thing: to live as faithful believers and followers of Jesus Christ.

As we begin this study, let's learn from James on how to apply our faith in practical steps. My hope is to help break things down so all of us have a better understanding about living through trials and tests when they come our way.

I don't know what kind of trial you may be going through right now. As I write this book, I am going through a particularly big one myself. But here's what I *do* know: God is the same yesterday, today, and tomorrow and I know He is sovereign and just. I also know He is still on the throne and hears my prayers. Breakthrough is going to happen! I can promise you that because our Lord God promises that.

Hang on and don't lose heart because there is a big difference between what is fact and what is *truth*.

CHAPTER 1

OUR FAITH AND OUR TRIALS

Reading assignment: James Chapter 1

Nothing becomes strong without testing it first.

One day, God was talking with a man and told him to push on a huge rock every day until He came back. God said that would be enough. "Do you promise to do this?" God asked. The man promised. So every day, faithfully, the man would push on the rock and try to move it. Two years went by, and after being faithful to push and move the rock, the man lost hope and got discouraged. He cried out to the Lord, "God, I have failed you! I have tried to move this rock every day for two years, just as you asked me to, but I can't! I have failed you, and I'm sorry." God answered the man, "My son, I never asked you to move the rock. I asked you to faithfully push on the rock and you have done precisely that. Now look at your body. It is strong, like that of a mighty warrior. That is what I have called you to do. You were faithful in pushing on the rock, but you caused yourself undue anguish when you began thinking I said to move the rock. You have not failed Me. You are now ready to serve Me the way I intended for you to. Now you are ready for what I have in store for you."

God calls us to a life of faith, and often we lose hope along the way because things didn't work out like we thought they should. Is your life one of obedience in your faith? Has God called you to push on a rock and you keep trying to move it instead? Take a moment and seek the Lord in prayer and ask Him if you changed direction and have re-written what He has asked of you? Write it down and pray over it. This will help bring clarity if you're struggling with confusion.

Just like the man in our story who became strong through the exercising of his muscles, our muscles too become toned through testing them when we exercise them. We get sore and struggle at first, but as we keep going the result is a stronger set of muscles and a healthier body.

> **God uses trials in our lives to help us mature spiritually.**

Trees are the same way. Trees develop a strong root system by enduring the strong winds that come from storms. Dirty coal changes into a beautiful and sought-after diamond by enduring intense pressure. And steel becomes strong through fire.[3]

Three types of trials

Trials come in many ways, but there are three main ones that appear often.

1. Outward trials—trials that build character.
2. Trials from Within—come in the form of temptations
3. Trials from the Word—require faith and how we choose to conduct ourselves.

#1. Outward trials:

> *"Consider it pure joy my brothers, whenever you face trials of many kinds because you know that the testing of your faith develops perseverance. Perseverance must finish its work so that you may be mature and complete, not lacking anything."*
>
> James 1:2-4

This does not suggest we should seek out trials. Nor are we to pretend that enduring trials is pleasant, because we all know it's not. We should however, look at trials as an occasion for joy because of the potential of producing something good in us. Sometimes God uses trials in our lives to purge or remove defects from our immature faith. I can assure you that

God will work through difficult circumstances in our lives to help us grow to full maturity.

> *"...in all things God works for the good of those who love Him."*
> Romans 8:28 (emphasis mine)

The process of gold becoming pure is an interesting one that is used as a metaphor for the Christian walk. You see, in order for gold to become pure, it has to go through a boiling process. As the impurities are brought to the surface and scooped out, the gold becomes more bright and reflective. It is only ready when the goldsmith can see his reflection in the gold—then he knows it is pure. That is the goal of the Christian walk. God matures us and removes the impurities of our lives as we endure testing and the result is Christ's face in us as a glorious reflection to the world—who desperately needs to see Him.

The Story of Joseph

Another example of an outward trial is the life of Joseph. The story is found in Genesis 37–47. Joseph endured the jealousy of his brothers who sold him as a slave and made it look like he was killed. That was complete rejection. Then, as he was working as a house servant for a rich man in Egypt whose name was Potiphar he found himself falsely accused of sexual immorality by Potiphar's wife and was immediately thrown in jail. He was rejected and falsely accused—that's a challenging trial!

After he had been in jail a while, the butler, whom he befriended, got out. Joseph asked the butler to remember him when he spoke to Pharaoh, but the butler forgot. It would be another two years before the butler remembered Joseph because of his gift to interpret dreams.

Joseph must have felt forgotten by God, just like we do at times.

Then Joseph was released to interpret a dream for Pharaoh that no one could interpret and his life changed dramatically with the snap of a finger after that. You must read the whole story to get the full affect, and I encourage you to do so, because it's really a good one.

Joseph, I'm sure, was confused concerning God's plan for him when he endured so many trials. Yet, he was able to come through these tests believing that God was working for the good. Rather than feeling the need to take revenge on his brothers (after he became the second most powerful man in Egypt) he said,

> "But God sent me ahead of you to preserve for you a remnant on earth and to save your lives by a great deliverance."
>
> Genesis 45:7

God used many trials to make Joseph mature and complete. We don't always see the bigger picture at work here. God used Joseph's life for this purpose of saving people from a famine. As the story of Joseph is winding down at the end of Genesis, Joseph says to his brothers (who now know who he is),

> "You intended to harm me, but God intended it for good to accomplish what is now being done, the saving of many lives."
>
> Genesis 50:20

Remember, there is always a bigger picture at work in our lives that we don't see. Trust God with your life and your circumstances. Surrender it to Him and have hope that there is something bigger around the corner. Remember, we are tested that we may grow.

Be obedient and faithful in what God is calling you to do, even it's just pushing on a rock. Pearls become pearls through agitation; it's only after that that they are beautiful and valuable. Trust in the timing and the process to mature.

In James 1:2 many translations say to "Count it all joy ..." The word "count" in the original Greek is used when keeping a business ledger and something is counted as a loss. James is telling his readers to logically acknowledge that God has allowed a trial to come into their lives to test their faith. A steadfast faith will benefit them later when future troubles come along. Knowing that, and with God's help, one can survive the hard times—which produce hope—and hope produces the joy.

Jesus Himself said, "In this world you will have trouble... (John 16:33)," but He also said He has overcome the world and He sent His Spirit to help us overcome it, too.

My point is—troubles, trials, and temptations will produce desirable results if we allow God to use them.

Having Wisdom

> *"If any of you lacks wisdom, he should ask God, who gives generously to all without finding fault, and it will be given to him."*
>
> James 1:5

Jewish Christians of the day would have understood wisdom. To James and the Jews, wisdom was much more than knowledge and intelligence. Judaism emphasized that "the fear of the Lord" was the starting point of wisdom.

Godly wisdom equips and enables us to live successfully by God's standards.

James urges his readers to ask God for insight to allow them to see the events of their lives from the divine perspective.

Later on, we'll look at the contrast between *earthly* wisdom and *divine* wisdom. But when dealing with divine wisdom, we can learn and understand that sometimes our trials can merge into God's plan for our lives.

So how do we get this wisdom? First, we must understand that God is a giving God. Giving to those who ask of Him is natural for God.

> *"Ask and it will be given to you; seek and you will find; knock and the door will be opened to you."*
>
> Matthew 7:7

But we have to ask first.

Second, God gives generously to all. He has no favorite recipients of His gifts, but gives to all classes and all races.

Third, God gives without finding fault. He does not give in such a way as to humiliate us. He does not chastise us for our failures or hold our unworthiness against us. He is always ready to add new blessings to us.

And fourth, God promises to answer those who come seeking wisdom. A request to Him according to His will receives His answer.

Our Faith and Our Trials

> *"This is the confidence which we have before Him, that, if we ask anything according to His will, He hears us. And if we know that He hears us in whatever we ask, we know that we have the requests which we have asked from Him."*
>
> 1 John 5:14-15

Godly wisdom equips and enables us to live successfully by God's standards. And we all need God's wisdom to cope successfully with life; but we should ask without wavering.

Our *attitude* is key when approaching the throne room of God. God must be approached with respect and with trust in His ability and His willingness to give us this gift of wisdom. God is not our friend, our "buddy" and should not be treated so casually.

He is a sovereign Lord, our King, and worthy of it all. Consider the posture of your prayers when you approach God.

When We Doubt

Work at not doubting either. Doubting makes you distrustful of God and it brings on instability in your thoughts. According to scripture it brings on a double-mindedness.

The situation that you are going through may be grim, but doubting God and not trusting Him makes *you* unstable in the circumstances, not the circumstances themselves.

> *"But when you ask, you must believe and not doubt, because the one who doubts is like a wave of the sea, blown and tossed by the wind ... Such a person is double-minded and unstable in all they do."*
>
> James 1:6, 8

Double-mindedness is when one part of a person that says, "Yes, that's true," and the other part says, "No, that is not true," which creates a painful inner turmoil in us. Therefore, God may be less likely to answer because He delights in answering prayers that are prayed with the simple faith of a child who knows his Father's will. God is a good God who loves you

Doubting God is serious.

and wants the best for you. We need to begin to run it through that belief system first before we can move on.

Let us be careful not to make light of our hesitant faith. Doubting God is serious. When we doubt like this, it's really implying that we have a low view of God. So, we need to be diligent in our prayers to Him. Hebrews 11:6 sums up my point best.

> *"And without faith it is impossible to please God, because anyone who comes to Him must believe that He exists and that He rewards those who earnestly seek Him."*
>
> Hebrews 11:6

Ask yourself, do I believe in a good, gracious, merciful, and faithful God? Do I believe He is sovereign and all-powerful? Can He *really* answer my prayers? Does He *really* care enough to get involved in my life and my problems? The answer is unequivocally, yes! But, we have to make up our minds about these things before we can pray with an earnest heart.

Here's my point—the more we study God's Word, the more He chooses to reveal Himself to us through it. So, good for you for seeking out a study for a deeper understanding! And I promise God will reveal Himself to you as you go along.

The Rich and the Poor

Being rich, poor, and even healthy can become challenging in the outer trials we face. James 1:9 addresses the poor and the rich and speaks of their material standing. The poor must not lament their poverty, but must rejoice at God's bounty in their lives.

There is a documentary I saw recently simply titled, *"Happy"*. It spotlights a handful of people who are and were in extreme circumstances, but found peace and happiness in the midst of it all. It's a great view of how we should look at our own circumstances in life despite what we see on the outside. It starts from within.

James speaks to the poor and encourages them to recognize their standing in God's sight. He goes on to say that the rich must not delight in their wealth but must find joy in the humility which trials produce in their lives.

Just because you have a lot of money does not mean you are exempt from trials. He reminds the rich of the necessity to be humble in spirit for their wealth withers quickly. Just remember the next time you drive by a junk yard. At one time those cars were someone else's dream car, all shiny, new and fresh off the assembly line. All of it eventually deteriorates, rusts, and withers away. So be careful not to hold on too tightly to your material possessions.

Life's trials do not discriminate whether we have a lot of money or not, or whether we're healthy or not.

Having Physical Health

Possessing physical health and material wealth should not produce pride either. We all should recognize that any of this cannot protect ourselves from life's circumstances. For example:

Steve Gleason was an outstanding professional football player for the New Orleans Saints. His career was on the top and things couldn't have been going any better for him. But then he was stricken with ALS (Amyotrophic Lateral Sclerosis). This is a slow and debilitating disease that will eventually take his life, and there is no cure as of yet. I happen to know a lot about ALS because my dad died of this awful disease in the early 1990's. With Steve's celebrity status, he brought attention and funding to this disease and created the "ice bucket challenge" that went through social media a few years ago to raise money and awareness for it. He was focusing on the greater good rather than just the physical situation he is was in. There is a movie out about him now and one of the captions to promote it read, "Steve Gleason was a football hero. Now, his legacy is teaching us how to love."

> Life's trials do not discriminate whether we have a lot of money or not, or whether we're healthy or not.

From my understanding, Steve is a believer in Christ. He is using his situation and celebrity status to catapult this disease to the forefront of our minds so we will give and become aware of it to help find a cure one day. But he also is using it to show others Christ's love. He is not choosing to focus on the external and what he doesn't have, but for what is eternal. Nothing in the world really matters except what is in the recesses of our hearts and what awaits us in eternity with the Father. That should be our focus, too. We can achieve much if we live by this perspective. God bless you Steve Gleason.

> *"Therefore we do not lose heart. Though outwardly we are wasting away, yet inwardly we are being renewed day by day. For our light and momentary troubles are achieving for us an eternal glory that far outweighs them all. So we fix our eyes not on what is seen, but on what is unseen, since what is seen is temporary, but what is unseen is eternal."*
>
> 2 Corinthians 4: 16-18

Pastor David Bramble, a local pastor in the Nashville area where I live, had a 17-year-old son whose life changed in an instant at a high school football game. He suffered a severe head injury during a game and has been in and out of hospitals and re-habs. The family has also endured additional trials with money, hospital bills, lawyers, etc. But he offers another definition of hope which I want to share with you.

> "Hope is a confidence of God, through faith in Christ; which is evident in times of uncertainty. It is when you have every reason and excuse to believe what is seen and heard, but cling to that which is eternal."
>
> ~Pastor David Bramble

This is not our home—remember that. God is good—remember that too. Trust Him for the bigger picture in your life.

#2. Inner trials:

In the midst of our outward trials we must resist the inner temptation to test God with complaints, grumblings, and various sins that arise from our doubting hearts, just as the Israelites did in the desert. Practically speaking, sin occurs whenever a person's mind approves the performance of a sinful act. Think about that. To fulfill these desires causes deception. Uncorrected deception leads to disobedience and sustained disobedience leads to death. Only good gifts come from God above.[4]

It's true that misery does love company—so listen closely to what people are saying to you with their grumblings and see if you hear the justifications for their sins.

South America is home to a vine known as the *matador*, which means, "killer." Beginning at the base of a tree, the vine slowly makes its way to the top. As it grows, it kills the tree, and when at last the top is reached, it sends forth a flower to crown itself.

Similarly, in the Christian life there are deadly vines known as *temptations*, which must be plucked from the roots at their earliest stages before they kill our spiritual lives.[5]

All of us at one time or another have given into temptations of some kind. Whether they are evil desires, deceptions, or disobedience—we have experienced it. And the result was a sapped spiritual life, right?

They say the first step to solving a problem is to recognize it. First, admit you have a problem with whatever it is you're being tempted with or acting out on. The second step is to bring it to God. God can supply both grace to endure and strength to resist. He uses our endurance and our resistance to give us spiritual maturity and growth in holiness and stamina. Humble yourself and repent. His grace is sufficient. Now hand it over to Him to help you take action steps to begin your journey toward healing.

You see, we are tested that we might grow.

#3. Tested by the Word:

I can't imagine getting through any kind of outward or inward trial without the Word of God to guide me. James discusses at least three subjects in his desire for Christians to heed the Word of God. He urges us to apply wisdom to our everyday life by being quick to listen and slow to speak. This means speaking thoughtfully and being slow to anger. Watch out to not be careless with your words.

> *"Everyone should be quick to listen, slow to speak and slow to become angry."*
>
> James 1:19

The Greek word for anger is *orge*, meaning "impulse, indignation, or wrath." Angry outbursts are to be avoided because they are irrational, unreasonable, and will do more harm than good. Human anger is usually concerned with self-interests and not righteous ones. To be angry at sin (concerned about the rights of others or the righteousness of God) is possible, but only as one grows in the Spirit of Christ. Anger itself is not a sin however, it's the motivation *behind* it that often is. What is the motivation of your heart when you flare up?

It is usually a self-serving, self-focused anger; and that is not good.

Different Kinds of Anger

We tend to think that the people who yell and lash out are the ones with the real anger problems. But there are other unhealthy ways to show anger too. For some it is the slow-burning fuse and others just stuff it way down inside of themselves. Whether you're stuffing the anger or letting it simmer this type of anger puts off the problem until later, but it will eat you up inside like a cancer if it is not dealt with.

Some people express anger with verbal darts (cutting remarks, unkind humor, or sarcasm). I've seen parents use this on their children. They are usually flippant remarks that are like arrows to the heart. This type of anger is eroding to the one receiving it. The one expressing it may feel better in the split-second they say it but what they say has a lasting effect on the one who's shouldering that poison. And sometimes it can last a lifetime. This is where the tongue has the power of life and death. Don't be careless with what comes out of your mouth.

> *"Words kill, words give life; they're either poison or fruit—you choose."*
> Proverbs 18:21 (MSG)

Many people also use the silent treatment. Studies have shown that this form of anger is one of the most damaging of all. It's rude, selfish and very cruel. It leaves the one receiving the silence to never know where they stand. There is no resolution and they are left to figure it out in isolation. This will affect them as they grow up because they will develop a distrust towards people and it will inhibit their social interactions too.

Still others keep long lists of grudges and offenses against people and refuse to forgive them. Unforgiveness can destroy your health. I've heard it said it's possible that unforgiveness can be some of the causes of fibroids and tumors that grow in us. We are not meant to carry the heaviness of unforgiveness, bitterness, and resentment. We're not designed for that so surrender it all to God! His yoke is easy (Matt. 11:30). Hand it to Him, because if you do you'll live longer.

> **Human anger is usually concerned with self-interests and not righteous ones.**

Not one but *all* of these types of anger are unhealthy and they need to change in us. There is a root problem that goes much deeper and it can be addressed through counseling and always through prayer. Take some time this week and reflect on yourself. If this is you and you're struggling with anger then begin to take action by asking for help from someone you trust and start changing any bad habits you may have in this area.

But the first step is admitting it and the second is taking it to Christ to repent. The third step is finding someone to help you walk this out.

The Art of Listening

James also warns against pretending instead of listening, deceiving instead of obeying, and talking instead of serving.

Some people go to school and half listen to lectures, and for some it's meetings at work. Meetings, lectures, and even sermons; we can learn to become listless listeners if we're not careful. A listless listener is someone who can endure a speech, a lecture, or a sermon without purposing to do a thing. We must be doers of the message of God's Word and not just hearers! Hearing the message without applying it leads to self-deception and developing a listening that produces no action or change but instead promotes hypocrisy.

> *"By this we may know that we are in Him: whoever says he abides in Him ought to walk in the same way in which He walked."*
> 1 John 2:6

Hearing the Word of God is necessary and important because our faith begins through hearing.

"Consequently, faith comes from hearing the message, and the message is heard through the Word about Christ."

Romans 10:17

James wants us to get this point.

"Do not merely listen to the word, and so deceive yourselves. Do what it says."

James 1:22

Hearing the Word of God is the preliminary steps to *obeying* the Word of God. By obeying the Word of God it can bring change, which is a good change in our lives.

If we're not growing we're atrophying.

We will all face trials in this life and we will face more trials of many kinds as we continue living out this life. So it's important that we seek God's wisdom and sovereignty in all of our situations—particularly those that bring negative emotions. Let's have a willingness to confess it all and lay it at His feet and know by doing that we will find peace and that will bring understanding.

Let's Review

When going through trials, consider your relationship with God as you realize;

1. The steadfast love of God *never* ceases
2. His mercies *never* come to an end
3. His mercies are new *every* morning
4. Great is His faithfulness[6]
5. He is our portion, so we will hope in Him.

God *wants* to bring us to a mature faith in Him so He can work wonders in our lives! Won't you let Him?

CHAPTER 2

PLAYING FAVORITES

Reading assignment: James Chapter 2

"My brothers, as believers in our glorious Lord Jesus Christ, don't show favoritism."

James 2:1

Trying not to judge or favor a person by external appearances may be harder than you think. Most of us, perhaps without even realizing it, do notice things like clothes, jewelry, cars, homes, etc, and allow what we observe to influence our opinions that we form of people.

As Christians we are taught to show compassion for the poor and the spiritually hungry—rather than cater to the powerful. A mature Christian relates to others with fairness, mercy, and acts of love.

But you may be asking how do we do this?

- By not showing favoritism,
- By choosing mercy over judgment,
- And by demonstrating our faith through action.

The believers in James' day fell into the same error we experience today: *favoritism* and *prejudice* based on things like a financial status of someone, or their skin color, or their position in society, etc. You name it, we've all experienced ourselves doing it, too. Just take a moment and fill in the blank.

If we're not growing we're atrophying.

The Early Church

The early church met in Jewish synagogues, which had special seats for those who were the most honored.

Here's an interesting point I want to share about how meanings of words have changed over time. For example: "Gay" really means to be happy. "Fag" is a tiring task and in Britain it means a cigarette. Those are just a couple of examples of words that now mean something different to our world culture. Sadly, one of them is a slur meant to be said in a hateful way. But that's not how it originated.

It is no different with the Old Testament and New Testament writers. The Greek word for "favoritism" is *prosopolempsia*, which literally means "to lift up one's face." Originally it was used for a king showing favor by literally lifting the face of a prostate beggar. Over time it came to mean "accepting a person instead of a cause," and then eventually it morphed into "a show of partiality."[7]

The Showing of Favoritism

In verse 3, James warns against giving the rich and favored people the good seats—showing partiality in the synagogues—while telling the poor to *sit on the floor* or *stand over there*. That is favoritism and he is saying not to do it.

Today, this still exists. People still cater to the celebrity status of people and cater to the money they have. Now, just to be clear here, the Bible does not condemn wealth. Sometimes we get off-track here and think that having money and being wealthy is a bad thing. It's not. Many men of God were rich beyond measure.

- *Abraham:* "Very rich in livestock, silver, and gold." Genesis 13:2
- *King Solomon:* "King Solomon exceeded all the kings of the earth in riches [wealth] and in wisdom." 1 Kings 10:23
- *Job:* "He possessed 7000 sheep, 3000 camels, 500 yoke of oxen, and 500 female donkeys, and very many servants, so that this man was the greatest of all the people of the east." Job 1:3
- *Joseph of Arimathea,* who wrapped Jesus' body in linen and laid Him in his own tomb. "…there was a rich man from Arimathea,

named Joseph, who also was a disciple…" Matthew 27:57
- *Zacchaeus*: "He was a chief tax collector and he was rich…" Luke 19:2

These are just a few examples. Money itself is not evil. We are taught it's the *love* of money is where we get into trouble. God is about the heart. God is always about the condition of the heart. What is your heart saying about the subject of money? Do you covet it? The Bible warns against the seduction of riches.

> *"For the love of money is a root of all sorts of evil, and some by longing for it have wandered away from the faith and pierced themselves with many griefs"*
>
> 1 Timothy 6:10

The Subject of Discrimination

James' concern was that Christians of that day, whether wealthy or not, were not ministering as Jesus had to the poor and the physically needy. Discrimination was rampant.

> **The world should see Christ through our actions as well as our speech. This is the fruit of Christ's Spirit.**

For example:

- Jews refused to communicate with the Samaritans.

> *"A woman of Samaria came to draw water."Give Me a drink," Jesus said to her, for His disciples had gone into town to buy food. "How is it that You, a Jew, ask for a drink from me, a Samaritan woman?" she asked Him. For Jews do not associate with Samaritans."*
>
> John 4:7-9

- Jews refused to associate with certain groups

> *The religious would not associate with misfits and sinners. "While He was reclining at the table in the house, many tax collectors and sinners*

came as guests to eat with Jesus and His disciples. When the Pharisees saw this, they asked His disciples, "Why does your Teacher eat with tax collectors and sinners?"

Matthew 9:10-11

- The wealthy ignored the pleas and pain of the poor.

"Now there was a certain rich man who was habitually dressed in expensive purple and fine linen, and celebrated and lived joyously in splendor every day. And a poor man named Lazarus, was laid at his gate, covered with sores. He [eagerly] longed to eat the crumbs which fell from the rich man's table. Besides, even the dogs were coming and licking his sores. Now it happened that the poor man died and his spirit was carried away by the angels to Abraham's bosom (paradise); and the rich man also died and was buried."

Luke 16:19-22 (AMP)

This story goes on to say that the rich man went to hell. His eyes were always on himself and he was never about others. I encourage you to go and read the whole story in Luke. It's a good lesson for us all.

Sadly, not much has changed in our times today. Do we look at the homeless people that beg on the street corners as sub-human? Do our eyes dart away when we see them at a stop light? The problem in America is so enormous that it overwhelms the mind and emotions. Common sense must dictate to some degree the place and extent of our involvement, but my point is—is there even a thought of involvement to start with?

Each of us whom God has blessed has the ability to do something.

Only you can answer if it is enough.

A while back I served at the church we were attending in a program called *Room at the Inn*. Room at the Inn was a program where churches in the area would set up cots and house the homeless during the frigid temperatures of the winter months. The homeless men would sleep over for a night and in the morning they were served breakfast and given a lunch to take with them. I came to help with the breakfast/lunch part.

I had the opportunity to sit and speak to a few of the men that would converse with me and I was surprised to meet some well-educated people who were just down on their luck. Not all homeless are *off their meds* or *crack-heads*. The Lord opened my eyes to my ignorance as I learned that these men had families. They were someone's child, brother, father. Through circumstances they had lost their way and some of them were in situations out of their control. They needed some encouragement, not judgment.

I'm sure it's humiliating to stand on the corner and beg. We don't know their circumstances and it's not for us to judge. However, we *are* to pray for them and give to them as the Lord leads us to give. My point is they are not sub-human. These are God's children, too, and they should not be made to feel forgotten. Just like us, they are hurting. Their pain just shows more.

James tells us to,

> *"Speak and act as those who are going to be judged by the law that gives freedom, because judgment without mercy will be shown to anyone who has not been merciful. Mercy triumphs over judgment!"*
>
> James 2:12-13

It's all about our heart's condition. How's the condition of your heart?

When We Show Mercy

The law was given not to condemn us but to point us to the need for a Savior—whom God expresses His grace through. If we condemn others because they don't measure up to our standards we should change our attitudes and be kind and merciful toward them just as God has been toward us. This is what James is telling us.

Remember the parable Jesus told of the unmerciful servant? It's found in Matthew 18:23-35. In this story, a servant could not repay the king a huge debt he owed back to him. It was more than he could earn in a lifetime. The king felt compassion for the servant and released him from prison and forgave the debt. Then the servant approached a fellow servant who owed him a mere hundred denarii, which was considered one day's wages. Because he couldn't repay it, this newly debt-free servant showed him no mercy and had him thrown in prison. The king was told of the incident and was angry! He asked the servant,

"Shouldn't you have shown mercy on your fellow servant just as I had on you?"

Matthew 18:33

The unmerciful servant was then punished unmercifully.

When we consider this story, we think of the unmerciful servant to be unbelievably hardhearted and cruel. But when we recognize that the King of the universe has forgiven us for a lifetime of transgressions and sins—how is it then that we harbor unforgiveness and judgmental attitudes toward our fellow servants? Even for such relatively small offenses that could fit into the course of a single day?

Let me ask you; who in your life do you need to forgive? It's time to stop carrying this and lay it down. It's doing you more harm than them. Take a moment and write down who you are struggling to forgive. Now go through your list one name at a time and ask God to help you forgive them. This is an act of obedience. You may not *feel* it right away but date it as you go through this exercise and remind yourself when the unforgiveness flares up; you have already forgiven them! You'll have the date there to remind you that you did forgive. Then let it go because it is not yours to carry anymore. You have laid it at the altar.

My aunt told me once, "share the Bible, and if you have to, use words."

> **A goal we should strive for is that others see Christ in our actions. We need to demonstrate our faith.**

Faith and Action

James argued that if faith is not accompanied by action, it is dead. This faith is not a saving faith involving the will, but it is just an emotional reaction and that is all. We must back it up with an action!

Understanding the truth intellectually is not enough. Even demons have an understanding of scripture and know who God is. Yet they fear Him more than we do! But the difference between us and them is they will continue in their rebellion towards God. Their actions reveal their rejection of Him. Do our actions reveal the same thing?

Faith without works is dead. So, take action toward your faith now.

Remember Jonah? He had a head for God but not a heart for God. He judged the very people he was sent to preach to. His story is found in the book of Jonah and I encourage you to read it.

If we truly believe Jesus died for us, then we cannot help but lay down our lives for others. The famous theologian, John Calvin, once said, "It is faith alone that justifies, but faith that justifies can never be alone."

Let's talk about being faithful. Here's a couple of examples the Bible gives us on what great faith looks like:

1. **Abraham** is mentioned as being faithful. It took great faith to put his son upon the altar—his *promised* son—and walk in obedience to God during that whole process. Abraham had faith even to the point of raising the knife on his son, Isaac!

2. **Rahab** is mentioned as faithful. She could have been killed by her own kind for hiding spies. But her motivation was believing in the God of Israel. She could have believed but not risked her life to help them either. Her action is why she is mentioned as one with great faith.

Recently, I saw a one-woman play about Corrie ten Boom, and the re-telling of her life story. I had read her book, *"The Hiding Place"* but the one-woman play brought forth more personal sides and the reality she had endured.

Her strength came from her father's teachings of God's Word. They knew the atrocities that were going on with the Jewish people in their country and they knew these were God's chosen people being persecuted. Jesus was a Jew also, and they loved and worshiped Him. So it made sense that they stood for and with all the Jewish people and decided to help them.

They made a choice as a family to act on faith and hide those Jewish families in spite of the scary circumstances. They hid as many as they could. They put Jewish babies to be raised with families far away from Germany so their lives would be spared. They put their faith into action because the Bible says to; even to the point of getting arrested, sent to prison camps, or being executed.

The whole time I was listening to this actress retell Miss ten Boom's story, I kept thinking and challenging myself—would I get involved that far if it were me?

We have to look beyond ourselves sometimes and see the world how God sees it. It's not just from our tiny self-minded perspective. It's when our eyes are on the eternal that we find the courage to act. This Psalm rings clear;

"The LORD is on my side; I will not fear. What can man do to me?"
Psalm 118:6

There is a fitting illustration on faith I found by commentator Donald Barnhouse;

"Doctrine and doing are like the two parts of salt: Salt in itself is composed of two poisons: sodium and chloride. If you were to take either of the poisons you would die. But if you combine them properly, you have sodium chloride, and that is common table salt—without which there is no savor for our food, and indeed, no life and health to our bodies." [8]

Faith and works go together. If you doubt that your works are demonstrating your true faith, the solution is not to try to work harder, but rather to humble yourself before God and ask Him to increase your faith and its fruit. Both our faith and our works are gifts from Him. Let's not measure ourselves before others but simply be sure we live in love—treating *all* people as equals before God, showing mercy and kindness in whatever ways God directs.[9]

> **Faith is not believing in spite of evidence, but obeying in spite of consequences.**

CHAPTER 3

THERE'S POWER IN THE TONGUE

Reading assignment: James Chapter 3

I was visiting my aunt many years back and she came out in a red blouse that looked absolutely stunning on her. I said, "Wow, Aunt Patsy you look amazing in that color! I love that on you. I don't think I've ever seen you wear red before."

She smiled and said, "I'm 75 years old and it's only been recently that I wore red again."

I know my expression must have been one of perplexity. She then quieted down in her countenance and said that when she was 16 years old she bought a red dress for a dance at school. She came out of her bedroom dressed and ready to go to the dance feeling so pretty. Then her father quipped and said, "You remind me of a cheap whore in that color."

She immediately went back, changed her clothes, and never wore red again. It took almost 60 years for her to have the courage to wear red again and not let that memory and the feeling associated with it haunt her.

James tells us;

"We should be quick to listen and slow to speak."

James 1:19

James drew this kind of wisdom from his knowledge of the Old Testament.

> *"When words are many, sin is not absent, but he who holds his tongue is wise."*
>
> Proverbs 10:19

King David cried out to God for his sake and said,

> *"Set a guard over my mouth, O LORD; keep watch over the door of my lips."*
>
> Psalm 141:3

Throughout scripture and even in our daily lives we see again and again that our tongues have the power to comfort or confuse, soothe or hurt, bless or destroy. Proverbs 18:21 tells us, "The tongue has the power of life and of death". Now that's something to be taken seriously.

This whole chapter makes a point that as we mature as Christians, so must our speech. Our speech matures by opening our hearts to God's wisdom and placing our tongues under His control.

We need to take our words seriously! Solomon warns us,

> *"The words of the reckless pierce like swords…"*
>
> Proverbs 12:18

There are countless talk shows, news shows, etc…, that are careless with their tongues. We get desensitized by hearing this over and over, and soon we begin to think that this is normal behavior! There is a reason it is called "shock T.V." or, "shock radio". We listen because we can't believe what we are hearing and yet, we still keep listening! It's like watching a car wreck in slow motion.

However, as we keep listening and watching in our disbelief it drives the ratings up and keeps this toxic behavior on our airwaves. These type of talk shows with the panels of men and women can be found 24/7 on any T.V. or radio station. It seems all they do is shout at each other for a chance to be heard over the

> **"A slip of the foot you may soon recover, but a slip of the tongue you may never get over."**
>
> ~Benjamin Franklin

other person. It's just chatter. It's just noise. There is no real depth to what they are saying. They just want to keep their ratings up so they will say and do anything to get your attention to keep you on that station.

Sadly, we look at these "self-appointed" know-it-alls as experts when in reality they are just celebrities. These people do real damage for the sake of ratings. It's all quite awful and yet we keep listening to them.

Paul warns us in his letters to Timothy about this;

> *"Avoid godless chatter, because those who indulge in it will become more and more ungodly."*
>
> 2 Timothy 2:16

The more we hear ungodly talk the more it becomes our normal. Just look at how ugly social media has become. Turn away from this influence by turning off your television set and changing your radio settings.

We become what we associate ourselves with.

Teachers and the tongue

James was addressing the teachers of the day and his focus was a warning to them. It was considered a high calling to be a teacher then and it is listed among the New Testament gifts to help build up the body of Christ.

> *"And God has placed in the church first of all apostles, second prophets, third teachers, then miracles, then gifts of healing, of helping, of guidance, and of different kinds of tongues."*
>
> 1 Corinthians 12:28

> *"So Christ himself gave the apostles, the prophets, the evangelists, the pastors and teachers, to equip his people for works of service, so that the body of Christ may be built up…"*
>
> Ephesians 4:11-12

It is understandable that the position of a teacher was coveted. Among the Jewish people the teachers were the rabbis and they were highly regarded.

In Jesus' day rabbis were the scholars and some were elected to serve in the Sanhedrin; the highest court of their nation. Because they were so highly respected they were consulted when questions arose about Jewish Law.

Teachers were highly regarded among the Greeks as well. The Greeks enjoyed exchanging views and thoughts on philosophy, politics, economics, and religion.

So, one can see why James is giving warning here. The ability to influence and impress was as desirable then as it is now. We should heed the same warnings today! James must have come across some incompetent and unworthy teachers in the newly-established Christian communities. These teachers were "self-appointed" rather than "God-appointed."

Today with the rise of new celebrity-teachers from our new found way to communicate through social media, we are seeing more self-appointed teachers than God-appointed ones. Be careful! Check their credentials and make sure they are theologically sound before you consider following them. Do your homework because in this day and age, you cannot afford to be gullible. A wolf in sheep's clothing is coming and he is the father of lies. He can work through all sorts of teachers and twist theology and truth on you so don't be deceived!

When Jesus spoke to the teachers of His day He spoke very candidly to them. Remember, they were *self*-appointed teachers and not *God*-appointed ones. He is speaking about the Pharisees here, and most of them had an attitude of entitlement which usually is a characteristic of anyone who appoints themselves into leadership positions.

Jesus warns,

> *"Beware of the teachers of the law. They like to walk around in flowing robes and love to be greeted with respect in the marketplaces and have the most important seats in the synagogues and the places of honor at banquets. They devour widows' houses and for a show make lengthy prayers. These men will be punished most severely."*
>
> Luke 20:46-47

Anytime we find ourselves in a position of influence we must take our words seriously and be deliberate about what we are saying.

We show our maturity by being slow to speak and controlling our tongue.

James warns believers that there is a responsibility that comes along with being a teacher.

"We who teach will be judged with greater strictness."
James 3:1

Handling God's Word should be done with integrity. Anytime we are sharing God's Word to anyone anywhere, we are in a place of influence so we are in fact, teaching! I'm not just talking about the formal teachers, but also parents, siblings, neighbors, bloggers, vloggers, etc. Make every effort to see that your lives match your words and handle it carefully.

Three Dangers of the Tongue

In chapter 3:3-6, James gives examples of how something so small can control us and do damage, too, like a bit for a horse, or a rudder for a ship, or even a spark to a forest fire.[10]

Let's break it down some.

#1 - A Horse's Bit

Self-talk can be the ruin of a man. Just like the bit for a horse is in the mouth to control the animal, self-talk controls our every thought and can eventually corrupt our whole person if we let it. It starts with the mind and what's deep in our thought life.

> **A person who can control their tongue can keep his whole body in check.**

Our job is to take control of that thought and learn how to recognize if that thought is from heaven or hell. Here's something that may help: any thought that does not inspire hope is *not* coming from heaven.

Taking our thoughts captive is sometimes easier said than done. When I get stressed I don't sleep much at night and I struggle to quiet my mind. What I have begun to do over the years is to go downstairs and begin to read Psalms first and focus on praising God's name. It helps me change my countenance toward the situation and ultimately, Him. This is where I begin.

Now, I'm not saying I'm dancing and singing. No, on the contrary!

Sometimes I'm crying and sobbing right through the praising. But what I do is read the Psalms *aloud*. What begins to take place is a shift in my spirit. The audible sound of my voice to my ears commands my wayward spirit to calm down. My spoken word of His Word has power. I know deep down in the depths of my soul the truth of God's Word—the fact that He does indeed love me, but most importantly He is sovereign and King. That's the truth I need! My feelings are all over the place and they can't be trusted, but I can begin with a truth, and *that's* a truth. God's Word says I'm loved by Him. Knowing and dwelling on that fact allows me to humbly go to Him and admit that I am having a hard time with whatever it is I am dealing with that is keeping me up.

It's either torment from the enemy—which I have the power and authority to overcome—or my pride of not letting go of something I want and I'm fretting over it. I eventually reach a point where I take those lying thoughts captive with laying out the facts of my situation and my feelings and surrender both of them over to my Savior through the speaking of His Word. It is only then that I am able to go back to bed, after I surrender to the One who can handle it.

When we're in a battle over something it's not always easy to take thoughts captive, but it is necessary for us to have victory. It's a process that we have to practice over and over and as we do this we get stronger in the Lord.

#2 - The Rudder of A Ship

Next, the rudder for a ship can control the direction it goes. Be mindful of what comes out of your mouth because it not only directs your thoughts, it *will* control the direction of your actions and your life. The thoughts start out small in size then begin to grow and guide our actions. And actions have the potential to achieve great results or great failure. And don't get so caught up in bad speech that you begin to curse your blessings, too. James is warning us to make wise choices with our tongue.

#3 - The Spark from a Flame

And last, there's the uncontrolled tongue. It is a source of great destruction! Just like a little flick of a flame can absolutely destroy a huge forest, a small misuse of the tongue can cause great pain to others and destroy relationships in the process. Take a look at the damage that bullying can do. Bullying is just one example of an uncontrolled tongue. The Bible says our tongues are:

> *"...itself set on fire by hell."*
>
> James 3:6

In the fourth grade, I had an experience that eventually involved all three. I had a teacher who was my math and reading teacher who spoke to the class to encourage them to read better. Sadly, she used me as the example. She was careless with her words. She said, "You don't want to be the slowest reader like Jill do you?"

> **By nature, the tongue can serve as a divisive tool, but by grace it can serve as a blessing!**

Her uncontrolled tongue was a spark in my life.

I remember feeling bad, embarrassed, and even stupid at that very moment. Right then I began to believe the lie that I must really *be* stupid. I reasoned that she was the teacher and after all, I was only in fourth grade. And for years after that I partnered with this lie through self-talk about myself.

I allowed this to have control over me and my actions. From that incident in the fourth grade do you know I never read a whole book until I was 36 yrs old?! I got through high school through cliff notes and help from friends.

That statement had a profound effect on me. It was a spark that became a flame that led to a bit that became a rudder. It rooted deep in my mind and caused me to feel inferior and worthless. It took years to undo that view of myself; all because of a careless word from someone.

Thankfully, we can control our tongues. If you've messed up, invite God in and ask for forgiveness. Paul gives us a great reminder;

> *"Let your conversation be always full of grace, seasoned with salt, so that you may know how to answer everyone."*
>
> Colossians 4:6

There's a story of a young man during the Middle Ages who confessed to a monk, "I've sinned by telling slanderous statements about someone. What should I do now?" The monk replied, "Put a feather on every doorstep in town." The young man did just that. He then came back to the monk wondering what else he could do. The monk said, "Go back and pick up all those feathers." The young man replied excitedly, "That's impossible! By now the wind will have blown them all over town." The monk said, "So have your slanderous words become impossible to retrieve."[11]

Sometimes, even if we think we're taking our words seriously, we speak criticisms that come in the form of sarcasms or gossip that slips in here and there. Criticisms and gossip whether small or big are still criticisms and gossip! We need to ask God to help us change.

> *"Do not let any unwholesome talk come out of your mouths, but only what is helpful for building others up according to their needs, that it may benefit those who listen."*
>
> Ephesians 4:29

Solomon gives us another reminder on this topic;

> *"The words of gossip are like choice morsels; they go down to the inmost parts…"*
>
> Proverbs 26:22

I once was in a leadership position over a team of people. Sadly, I had allowed sarcasm to reign in some in our conversations. In reality, I hadn't recognized that the sarcasm was really criticism hiding behind sarcastic remarks. It began with underhanded compliments that were nervously laughed off. And over time, it began to plant seeds of doubt in my leadership abilities.

It was all very subtle and slow. Eventually and sadly, that led to gossip behind my back and it wasn't long after that I was full of self-doubt and not leading the way I knew was called to lead and walk in my gifting as a leader.

I didn't have the support I should have had and eventually it led to the demise of the whole team and organization we had built up together. What a painful lesson that was! It just takes a little yeast to get through the whole batch. It can go down to the inner most parts and it will bear rotten fruit that destroys. Lesson learned.

Wisdoms

There are two different types of wisdom: Earthly Wisdom and Heavenly Wisdom.

- *Earthly wisdom* comes from man and man alone. It is unspiritual and it usually comes from the devil himself. It shows signs of envy, selfish ambition, and brings about disorder, which ultimately brings about division—and that's the enemy's ultimate goal. Remember those talk shows I mentioned earlier? They certainly don't sow in peace. It's all about divisiveness that brings up the ratings.

In Proverbs it says,

"A perverse person stirs up conflict…"

Proverbs 16:28

Turn off those toxic shows and stay away from toxic people.

- *Heavenly Wisdom* is free from self-interest and strife. In chapter 3:17, James lists eight traits or characteristics of pure wisdom. They are: Pure, Peace Loving, Considerate, Submissive, full of Mercy, Good fruit, Impartiality, and Sincerity.

> **What goes down in the well comes up in the bucket.**

If our hearts are controlled by the *"wisdom that comes from heaven* (referencing 3:17)*"*, then our thoughts and emotions will be filtered and shaped into words that bless and encourage others as well. Are you using your tongue as an instrument to encourage others? I hope so.

Our lives are much like the computers we use today. How a computer is programmed determines how it is to function.¹² It is full of data that's put into it, and it's the same with our brains, too. If we are putting in junk, then we are putting out junk.

True wisdom results in a harvest of righteousness and that is by conforming to God's will; and God's will brings peace! It will always bring peace. So, if you aren't experiencing any peace in your life, then take a moment to identify what junk is in your life that you are allowing to "download" into your spirit. Ask the Holy Spirit to help you identify it—and then get rid of it. Jesus was speaking to the Pharisees about themselves and He said,

Words have power!

> *"You brood of vipers, how can you who are evil say anything good? For the mouth speaks what the heart is full of."*
>
> Matthew 12:34

An old saying says it this way: "What goes down in the well comes up in the bucket."

Words have power!

With social media around, we can easily slide into the habit of using our tongues and our fingers to communicate to belittle others. It may not be the *spoken* word that literally comes out of our mouth, but it is in our thoughts and our fingers nowadays that do the talking for us. Through our computers, we work out our own agenda that nobody can call us out on at the time we post it. Half the things we say, we'd *never* say to someone's face! With no accountability, we end up developing pockets of strife, promoting our policies, and justifying our actions. That's when things get ugly and we end up hurting those around us. We need to love peace and learn to respond in gentleness because through that we demonstrate mercy. Wouldn't we want someone to demonstrate mercy to us if we got ahead of ourselves?

A few years back, a famous comedian from the 1960's passed away. I was reading some online magazines about his death. One magazine posted this: "He tried to sue us and lost, so now look who's laughing!" That was the title of the article about his death!

What an awful and careless thing to say. We hide behind our little screens of blue light, thinking we are all-powerful with our own opinions. We convince ourselves that what we have to say matters to the world and we regurgitate them out (thinking only of ourselves at that moment) and forget demonstrating any kind of love or mercy at all—hurting people in the process. Whoever wrote that article and allowed that title was only thinking of themselves and not thinking of the grieving relatives that it will hurt.

Jesus' words are a reminder of what is really going on,

> "...*For the mouth speaks what the heart is full of.*"
>
> Matthew 12:34

God is always about the heart. What is your heart full of? Ephesians 4:29 is worth repeating:

> *"Do not let any unwholesome talk come out of your mouths, but only what is helpful for building others up according to their needs, that it may benefit those who listen."*

Commentator Thomas Lea summed it up this way,

> "We can do no better than to commit our tongues to the Lord, ask Him to develop true wisdom in us, and daily let Him refine and purify our flashes of selfishness, anger, resentment, and pride."

Ask Him for help to do so. Ask Him daily!

Only the grace of God can tame the tongue.

CHAPTER 4

FINDING HUMILITY

Reading assignment: James Chapter 4

"True humility is not thinking less of yourself; it is thinking of yourself less."

~C. S. Lewis

We all want to strive to live a godly life, right? But sometimes our commitment to that godly life is seriously challenged by our personal struggles with pride and envy. We struggle having trouble with other people because we sometimes are influenced by people who are covetous, quarrelsome, and judgmental. We have trouble with ourselves as well because we are naturally motivated by selfish desires and so we conform to the world's value system.

Submitting to the Lord and deferring others may not be popular in today's culture, but in the eyes of God, they are important skills to have. It's called humility.

Biblical humility is not weakness, but strength!

We need to find in ourselves a humility that exists toward God, toward others, toward our desires, and even toward our future.

During James' time, the Greek moralists gave little worth to the word, "humble." But James and the other New Testament writers drew from the riches of their Hebrew heritage, and over time actually changed the status of this word in the Greek vocabulary.

In its essence, to have humility means, "to be low." This is in contrast to pride, meaning "to be lifted high." Those who know God recognize it to be the greatest part of wisdom which is a characteristic of Christian maturity.[13] For it is lowering ourselves into the strong hands of our mighty God.

When We Quarrel

James begins this chapter with some questions

> *"What causes* quarrels *and what causes* fights *among you? Is it not this, that your* passions *are at* war *within you?"*
>
> James 4:1 (emphasis mine)

I emphasized certain words in this passage to give us a greater understanding of what James is saying. The Greek word for "quarrels" is *machai,* meaning "dispute, contention, or controversy." The Greek word for "fights" is *polemoi,* meaning "combat or battle." Then James mentions "passions." He uses the Greek word *hedonon,* which means "desires and/or sensual lusts," and for "war" the word used is *strateuo,* which means "to battle, carry on a military campaign." [14]

So now, let's repeat James 4:1 with the meanings put in;

> *"What causes* disputes, contention, controversies *and what causes these* combats *and* battles *among you? Is it not this, that your* desires *and* sensual lusts *are like a* military campaign *that you carry on within you?"*

Understanding these Greek words through this verse makes it obvious that the problems mentioned are deep-seated and serious. The point he is making is that the confrontations we have with other people are not just little disagreements; they are a real battle raging within the human heart that overflows into our relationships.

Is there a desire for combat from a controversy that breeds a desire for a battle? That is what this scripture is saying. Anger can be a motivator, but it is a destroyer in the end. Take the temperature of your heart. Pause, think, breathe, then speak and only then, begin to take an action—you'll be glad you did.

Remember, our context here is that James is speaking to Christians who show favoritism based on what a person possesses.

These are people who are sound in their doctrine, but weak in their duties. They are the ones who cannot control their tongues and who appoint themselves into teaching positions.

Do you know anyone like that? I do.

Remember James ended Chapter 3 with thoughts of peace stating that,

> "...a harvest of righteousness is sown in peace by those who make peace."
>
> James 3:18

But now in Chapter 4 he begins to talk about war and the poor condition of the human heart. James is speaking of what is going on between believers and within believers. These fights and disagreements are as offensive to God just as much as killing is!

Think about how often fellowship is mentioned among believers, and yet how seldom it is realized. God wants us to experience the kind of love the Holy Spirit makes possible. As the world grows more intensely opposed to God's people, the more we are going to need each other's support. James calls us to love each other and be peace makers, not warmongers.

Hostility Towards Believers

The hostility between believers is heartbreaking to God and a poor evangelistic witness to the world.

I remember back in the late 1980's there were two televangelists arguing on a late-night news show that was very popular at the time. They were being interviewed because one of the evangelists had "fallen from grace," and the other one waved his Bible and pointed his finger at the fallen evangelist. The ratings for this show when these two were on were some of the highest the show had seen.

Later on, they brought on another well-known televangelist that said this about the fallen evangelist—and I quote: "He's a liar, an embezzler, a sexual deviant, and the greatest scab and cancer on the face of Christianity in 2,000 years of church history!"

Regardless of the details, these comments and behavior should have never been aired for the nation to see. The comments were inflammatory and excessive. I remember being so embarrassed because it brought my identity as a Christian down in my unbelieving friends eyes. My unbelieving friends were even embarrassed! I remember how I grieved in my heart that this circus had been created in the news because these men, these pillars of the church, let their tongues fly free. And they did it all in the name of Jesus!

It was awful and I remember wondering how God must have been feeling about this. We can't expect people who don't know Christ to act any better, but we *do* expect men of God, or anyone proclaiming to be a Christian, to act better and above the rest because they are representing Christianity for all of us. I'll say it again; *Hostility between believers is a heartbreak to God and a poor evangelistic witness to the world.*

James goes on in this chapter to say that the people lacked what they sought because they failed to ask God. They wanted satisfaction, but they looked in the wrong places for it. They did not ask God as Jesus had taught them. They allowed their lives to be governed by pleasure, selfishness, and greed.

> *"You ask and do not receive, because you ask wrongly, to spend it on your passions."*
>
> James 4:3

God is about the condition of your heart. How is the condition of your heart? Can an unbelieving world tell that you are a follower of Jesus Christ?

We Need To Pray With Humility

Prayer without proper motivation does not move God to act. Yet the Bible is full of many examples for us to pray and many promises of God's responses. If we pray and nothing happens we get discouraged and stop praying. Then we get mad at God for not answering us. Don't you think it would be easier and even sensible to blame our faulty prayers than to blame a faithless God?

Author R.V.G. Tasker wrote:

> "There is, to be sure, no prayer that we all need to pray so much as the prayer that we may love what God commands and desire what He promises."

Again, what is the attitude of our heart when we go to God and pray? God is about the heart.

We need to humble ourselves before God in constant prayer, asking Him to heal our hurts and enable us to be peacemakers.

> *"Blessed are the peacemakers, for they will be called children of God."*
> Matthew 5:9

When we have true humility toward God then we are resisting the devil. This only happens when we are repentant toward our Creator.

This is not the outward humility that we have seen; that is a show. It is only another way of seeking praise and recognition from people and not God above. It's one of pride's most subtle masks, but it is pride nonetheless.

True humility is an open door to God's grace.

Sometimes we try to humble ourselves by needlessly punishing ourselves in private or in public. That's not humility either. God is not about embarrassing us to humble us. Don't buy into that because that's false humility.

The sign of true humility is that we don't really care what people think about us (in a good way) or our reputation. We only care about what God thinks of us and our character more. Our desire is to please Him first and foremost above all the rest.

Danny Wuerffel said this upon winning the Heisman Trophy in 1996:

> "First and foremost, I give all the glory to God. He is the rock on which I stand, and I would publicly like to ask Him to forgive me for my sins, of which there are many."

A man with a humble heart is more concerned of what God thinks of him than what man thinks of him. Even with all the success he had just achieved, Danny Wuerffel had the right perspective.

"Humble yourselves before God, and He will exalt you"
James 4:10

James wants us to learn to humble ourselves toward others, too. Be happy for others successes and don't entertain feelings of envy and pride. That just means your focus is back upon yourself.

There once was a famous conductor of a great symphony orchestra who was asked which instrument was the most difficult to play? He thought for a moment and then replied, "The second fiddle. I can get plenty of first violinists, but to find someone who can play the second fiddle with enthusiasm—that's a problem. And if we have no second fiddle, we have no harmony." [15]

> **We all play an important role in God's kingdom, so don't compare your life with others.**

The Problem with Comparing

When we compare our lives with others we let doubt override our thoughts because we think we don't measure up. We let pride seep into our thoughts thinking we're better than others. With social media around, now we can also look at other people's lives and wish we had their life, their home, their cars, or their vacations, etc… But that plain and simple; is envy and idolatry.

If you are stalking someone and what they wear, how they live, what their lives are all about, then that's idolatry because you are consumed with that rather than God. If you are the one doing all of the posting of your life, just make sure your heart is not one of pride and boastfulness saying, "Look at me! Aren't I great?" Because one is boastfulness, the other is idolatry, and both are rotten. Here's what the Word of God has to say about pride;

To fear the Lord is to hate evil;
I hate pride and arrogance, evil behavior and perverse speech.
Proverbs 8:13

Here's what the Word of God has to say about idolatry:

"You shall have no other gods before Me…"

Exodus 20:3

That's pretty clear. So ask yourself: what are you putting before God? Do your postings of prayers come to Facebook before they go to God? Do you lay out your daily agenda before bringing God in and asking Him? Do you find yourself worrying about the future and not trusting God for all your needs? Do you have a death grip on your possessions? Are you putting your faith and trust in those things first rather than God? Luke recorded a parable that Jesus used on this subject;

"The ground of a certain rich man yielded an abundant harvest. He thought to himself, 'What shall I do? I have no place to store my crops.' Then he said, 'This is what I'll do. I will tear down my barns and build bigger ones, and there I will store my surplus grain. And I'll say to myself, "You have plenty of grain laid up for many years. Take life easy; eat, drink and be merry."'

"But God said to him, 'You fool! This very night your life will be demanded from you. Then who will get what you have prepared for yourself?' This is how it will be with whoever stores up things for themselves but is not rich toward God."

Luke 12:16-21

As we humble ourselves toward God we will be able to take a humble stance regarding our future and then begin to rest in the fact that God is in control of it all. All of it! It's really a matter of trusting in Him and not trusting in what we possess. How much do you trust Him with your life right now?

When We're Anxious

If you are anxious about your future don't be. Cast all of your anxieties on Him (1 Peter 5:7). Bow to the Lord in humility and lay your cares at His feet. He loves you and will care for you—but you have to decide whether to trust Him first or not. That choice of trusting God lies only with you.

If we formulate our plans as if God doesn't exist or isn't worthy of being consulted, we aren't professing Christians, but practicing atheists

There was a pilot of a small passenger airplane carrying four people who suddenly yelled, "All out, we're going to crash! There's one parachute for each of us—follow me!" He put on a parachute, opened the emergency door and jumped, accidentally knocking another parachute out the door with him. The three remaining men stared at each other in shock. One, a middle-aged man, jumped and boasted, "I'm one of the smartest men in the world. Better to have a whole college of professors, or ten thousand scientists die than me!" He was quickly out the door. A minister and a young student remained. The minister spoke next with tears in his eyes, "Well, my lad, you should hurry and get that last parachute." The boy responded, "Relax Pastor. The smartest man in the world just jumped out of the plane strapped into my school bag!"[16]

Whatever our problems are, our solution is found in humbly submitting ourselves to God as we seek His guidance. The heart has to posture itself in humility as we enter into the King's presence.

"When pride comes, then comes disgrace, but with humility comes wisdom."
Proverbs 11:2

In Proverbs 16:8 it says, pride comes before the fall. So if this is true, let's just make sure our posture toward God Almighty is so low that we have nowhere to fall.

God exalts those who humble themselves before Him.

CHAPTER 5

ATTITUDE ADJUSTMENTS

Reading assignment: James Chapter 5

> "There is nothing that makes men rich and strong but that which they carry inside of them. Wealth is of the heart, not of the hand."
>
> ~John Milton

In this chapter James is addressing our attitudes. He focuses on our attitudes towards our wealth, our pain, being patient, and our prayers. He begins this chapter by challenging those who are irresponsible with their wealth. Remember earlier in Chapter 2, when James warned believers about courting the wealthy? Here he is addressing the privileged people who are taking advantage of the ones who are poor and helpless.

> **The possession of money does not make people evil any more than the lack of it makes people virtuous.**

Again, God does not condemn the wealthy. Remember God blessed men such as Abraham, David, Solomon, and even Job to be very wealthy men of God. It's the love of money that is condemned and not the money itself.

And that brings me to our attitude toward wealth.

Our Attitude Toward Wealth

The relevant points here are how the money was acquired and how it was being used. James accuses those in management of defrauding the poor.

They were increasing their wealth at the expense of those less fortunate. James knew the law of the Old Testament:

> *"Do not defraud or rob your neighbor. Do not hold back the wages of a hired worker overnight."*
>
> Leviticus 19:13

The law also states:

> *"Do not take advantage of a hired worker who is poor and needy, whether that worker is a fellow Israelite or a foreigner residing in one of your towns. Pay them their wages each day before sunset, because they are poor and are counting on it. Otherwise they may cry to the Lord against you, and you will be guilty of sin."*
>
> Deuteronomy 24:14-15

If we are fortunate to have wealth, what is our attitude about the people who work for us?

Our Attitude as the Employer

When I made my living as a singer years ago, I worked in the Christian, Country and commercial parts of the business. More times than I care to count, I had to chase down money owed to me when I worked for Christian vendors.

There was also a rate of pay that had been established for the Christian industry that was considerably less than the regular rate of pay for other work. That always perplexed me. Did that mean my family should eat less or that my bills should be less simply because I am a Christian?

Does a lawyer who becomes a Christian start charging a lesser rate because he's a Christian lawyer? Or should a Christian doctor do the same?

The worst of it for me was when I worked for secular vendors and they would find out I was a Christian. Once that happened, I was bombarded with questions like, "Why don't *you people* (meaning Christians) pay on time? Why do *you people* take advantage of workers?" When Christians behave poorly we all pay for it. It becomes a sad witness for Christians everywhere.

I bring this up only as an example to challenge our attitudes toward providing services. Be good to your workers and pay what is owed them and on time. That's just an example of treating others fairly. It will make a good witness for all.

The Rich and Their Attitude

Let's go back to James and the attitude of the rich. James begins this chapter criticizing the rich;

> *"Now listen, you rich people, weep and wail because of the misery that is coming on you. Your wealth has rotted, and moths have eaten your clothes. Your gold and silver are corroded. Their corrosion will testify against you and eat your flesh like fire. You have hoarded wealth in the last days. Look! The wages you failed to pay the workers who mowed your fields are crying out against you. The cries of the harvesters have reached the ears of the Lord Almighty. You have lived on earth in luxury and self-indulgence. You have fattened yourselves in the day of slaughter."*
>
> James 5:1-5

The words "wealth" or "riches" in those days were meant for grain, garments, gold, or silver. The descriptions that James uses are precise:

"Your wealth has rotted..." He is referring to agricultural products such as grain that rot easily in that climate.

"...and moths have eaten your clothes." All clothing can be destroyed by moths.

"Your gold and silver are corroded." All metals were usually stored together, so gold and silver corroded quickly when combined with base metals.[17]

When James says, *"Their corrosion will testify against you..."*—it seems to say it all.

This kind of disintegration occurs because of hording and disuse for their day of judgment is coming. Using stern language here, James is trying to shake the reader's faith in the worldly things they have become accustomed to and their all too comfortable attitudes towards them. They are not exercising the character traits James is wanting. They have become too comfortable and their riches are corroding.

All who believe in Christ, rich or poor, will enter heaven with empty pockets.

Here is a prime example of wealth misused. Hetty Green was known as the "Witch of Wall Street" and the richest woman in America during the gilded age (1870-1900). But she was also one of America's greatest misers.

Hetty was an only child born into a wealthy whaling family in 1834. Because her mother was too sickly and fragile to help raise her, her father and grandfather saw to her care. They trained her to handle money shrewdly from a young age, reading her stock market reports as other parents read bedtime stories.

She became a financier. She knew how to work numbers! She was considered by many to either be a brilliant strategist or a ruthless loan shark.

> It is wiser to store treasures in heaven by treating each person as an equal.

Hetty's audacity was apparent early on. When her aunt, Sylvia Howland, died in 1868 and left $2 million to charity, Hetty was incensed. She challenged the will in court, presenting what she claimed was a previously written will that left everything to Hetty. She lost the case.

She had two children and they wore cast-off clothes. Hetty, people said, had one dress and it was worn and tattered. She was so intent on saving money she would eat her oatmeal cold to avoid the expense of heating it.

Her son once fell down the stairs and hurt his leg badly. They went to the Dr.—the free clinic that is! They immediately recognized her and demanded payment. She left deciding it would heal on its own with the help of Carter's liver pills and oils. It did not. Later, while visiting his father, the boy fell again, and his father took him to the doctor. The leg was so bad it had to be amputated!

Since she kept their finances separate the father had to pay the expenses rather than go through the ordeal of haggling over it. Hetty's son lost his leg because she was too stingy to pay for proper medical care.

After 20 years of suffering a hernia, Hetty finally allowed Dr. Henry S. Pascal to examine her in 1915. When she disrobed down to her "old and none too clean" underwear, Pascal saw that she did indeed have a severe, bulging hernia. Her solution had been to jam a stick against the swelling, held in place by her underwear and the pressure of her own leg. The doctor told her that the extremely painful hernia needed an immediate operation. When he told her the cost, $150, she scowled and picked her fallen stick off the floor, replacing it in her underwear. She yelled, "You all are robbers!" and walked out.

Hetty died in 1916, leaving her fortune to her son and daughter. Her son lived a lavish life after her death and when he died in 1936 he left the majority of his money to his sister. When she died in 1951 she gave all of the amassed fortune to charity. It was $443 million dollars! [18]

> **Everyone has faith. The question is what are you putting your faith in?**

What a sad story of a life wasted by greed and fear.

"We brought nothing into the world, and we can take nothing out of it."
1 Timothy 6:7

Writer Luci Swindoll summed it up this way;

"The "good life" is not attaining a college degree, succeeding in your career, owning an expensive car, having money in the bank, or vacationing in Hawaii—although these are wonderful and sweet to my worldly tastes, it is not the "good life."

The Good Life is peace—knowing that I was considerate instead of crabby, that I stood by faithfully when all the chips were down for the other guy, that I sacrificially gave to a worthy cause, that I showed impartiality when I really wanted my preference, that I was real in the midst of phonies, that I was forgiving, that I had the courage to defer reward for something better down the road."[19]

Having a mature faith requires us not to look to the world's material pleasures for our true wealth.

An Attitude of Patience

Let's look at our attitude toward pain and patience. As we move on with Chapter Five, James reminds us to have patience in the challenges that life brings. He encourages us to exercise our patience. We tend to act impetuously at times, disregarding the consequences. Let me remind you that our loving God always acts at the right time for the right purpose. He does not work in our understanding of time and His perspective is much wider and broader than we can ever imagine. It's a matter of trust first and patience will follow.

He gives us the example of the farmer and how patient he has to be to wait on the fall and spring rains for his crops. It is the same for us—the harvest time of this world is coming! We must be patient to wait on God and His timing of it all.

Patience really is a virtue.

Being patient and steadfast while we wait on God is perhaps the most difficult of all. The disciplines God uses in our lives to conform us to the image of His Son take time because He is patience personified. Our goal in life is not to get to heaven all disheveled and a mess. Our goal is to become more Christ-like as we journey towards heaven. So exercising patience is just one step closer to becoming more like Christ.

Isaiah also encourages us to be patient.

> *"Yet the Lord longs to be gracious to you; therefore He will rise up to show you compassion. For the Lord is a God of justice. Blessed are all who wait for Him!"*
>
> Isaiah 30:18

Do we really think that the Lord might come back any day? He might. How easy it is for us to forget this.

Perhaps we should post a note to ourselves in a place where we'll see it daily—a small sign that says, "Am I ready?" Use it as a reminder to stay alert on how to live. Grab a Post-it note and put it on your mirror. See if this helps you as you begin your day.

Our Attitude In Speech

James also makes an important statement to not swear, that's a given. But he also wants us to be sure when we give our word to someone- that it is *reliable*. Let your "yes" be yes, and your "no" be no. Jesus used these same words in the Sermon on the Mount in Matthew chapter 5.

He was not talking about making a solemn oath to someone—that is different. For example, like swearing of an oath in a courtroom, or making a marriage vow, etc. It's not that.

Jesus is talking about swearing by sacred things in a flippant way. I need to state these to make a point, so forgive me if this offends anyone. But when we say things like, "I swear to God!" or "Jesus Christ!" or "For Christ's sake!", just to name a few, these are sacred and we should never, *ever,* take them lightly. Don't be careless with your mouth.

If you are a professed follower of Christ and you defame His name with these phrases, you dishonor yourself and God to an ungodly world who is going to judge you for it. Being a Christian is setting the bar higher because we follow the Most-High God. He is worthy of praise, honor, and glory! Keep your word and watch what you say. It's a huge witnessing tool when you do and the result will be that God will be honored.

Our Attitude and Integrity

I remember when my husband, Steve, was working as a recording session drummer. He would get called throughout the day to get booked for upcoming sessions. Some sessions paid great and some we were just thankful to get paid something.

He got a call one morning to help out a friend on a session that was coming up that next week. The pay was not great, but we needed the work and he wanted to help his friend, so he said yes. The next morning, he got a call for a session, the same day as the session that was booked the day before for twice the money!

I have to be honest, I was encouraging him to drop the first guy because all I could see was the money and paying bills with it. But Steve told me that his word was his word and his reputation for keeping his word was a bigger deal. Plus, it honored God, and God was going to have to fill in the blanks for the money. He calmed me down and he turned down the offer for that bigger session. Steve is a man of honor and integrity. And you know what? We never starved, the bills got paid because more work came in, and my faith grew because of what I witnessed.

> Temptation and testing are two sides of the same coin.

Don't be tempted to throw it all out because something looks better.

God expects us to fulfill our promises just as He does, so keep your word.

Our Attitude and Prayer

Now regarding our attitude toward prayer: prayer is a privilege. We get to talk to God about anything and everything. We can talk to Him if we're in trouble, if we're happy, sick, or in need of confessing something to Him. He is there. When it comes to prayer, it seems we have two main problems or road blocks that plague us. We either don't pray or we don't believe God hears our prayers, but that's simply not true. He is always listening and when He is silent, as hard as that is to endure, we have to trust there is a reason for it. But don't stop praying and talking to Him because His answer is coming.

A pastor was once asked, "Is it OK to pray about the little things in life?" He responded, "Madam, can you think of anything in your life that is big to God?"[20]

When we do pray, do we have faith enough that He hears us?

This is one of my favorite examples of faith in our prayers:

Once, a church called a prayer meeting because the drought in their area was becoming severe. As they were about to begin the meeting, the adult and elders of the church laughed with joy—and shame—when a young girl walked into the meeting; she was the only one who had the simplicity of faith to bring an umbrella!"[21]

Have an open communication with God. When we're suffering under pressure, we should let God know of our condition and seek help from Him. When things go well, we are encouraged to praise God by singing songs of praise to Him. He is worthy of all our praises! That's why I like journaling so much. It's a deliberate time that I take just for me and God. I write down my prayers, my praises and my dreams to Him.

> You can't out run God's ability to forgive.

It feels intimate for me and builds that relationship with my heavenly Father.

As I pour out my heart to Him, He speaks with me through the Holy Spirit and as this becomes more frequent, I am able to distinguish His voice as He talks to me and leads me. I can't encourage this enough for you to get in the habit of doing. Confess it all and talk to Him because He loves you and wants to hear from you too!

If you feel you're too unworthy to even go to God because of past sins, I want you to remember what Beth Moore has said;

"You can't out run God's ability to forgive"

If you are experiencing a distant feeling from God right now, remember that God is never distant from you. When you sincerely seek His presence He will touch you and restore your soul.

> *"When doubts filled my mind, Your comfort gave me renewed hope and cheer."*
>
> Psalm 94:19

"Doubting may temporarily disturb, but it will not permanently destroy your faith in Christ."

~Charles Swindoll

An Attitude of Thanksgiving

Prayer is a natural communication with Almighty God. Pray to Him with a heart of thanksgiving. Make this your first priority as you go to Him because this will set our countenance and our heart right with our King and Redeemer. Then make your requests known to Him.

> *"… by prayer and petition, with thanksgiving, present your requests to God."*
>
> Philippians 4:6(emphasis mine)

Paul has the best reminder for us to keep in mind;

> *"Be joyful always; pray continually; give thanks in all circumstances, for this is God's will for you in Christ Jesus."*
>
> 1 Thessalonians 5: 16-18

As we complete our study of the book of James, I hope this helps you to better understand how the use of our tongue, the attitudes we should carry, and the humility we need to exercise, are tools to help live successful lives and to help keep us moving forward as we encounter difficult trials. Living our lives as mature Christians consists of moment to moment decisions. Understanding the practicality of what James points out to us is the key to living a more peaceful and mature life in Christ.

We should always be moving forward with Him. I said this in an earlier chapter and it bears repeating;

**We are either growing or we are atrophying.
Don't stop growing.**

The Book of Job
The Example

JOB'S CHALLENGES

Some believe that Job is a mythical figure and that he really didn't exist. But to believe this, means that we would have to omit other portions of the Bible that reference his life.

When Ezekiel is speaking for God and he lists Job as a true historic and righteous person along with Noah and Daniel.

> *"Or if I should send a plague against that country and pour out My wrath in blood on it to cut off man and beast from it, even though Noah, Daniel and Job were in its midst, as I live," declares the Lord GOD, "they could not deliver either their son or their daughter. They would deliver only themselves by their righteousness."*
>
> Ezekiel 14:19-20

James mentions Job as a man persevering.

> *"As you know, we count as blessed those who have persevered. You have heard of Job's perseverance and have seen what the Lord finally brought about. The Lord is full of compassion and mercy."*
>
> James 5:11

You see, Job was a real person. He was a real-life man who was married, the father of ten children (and eventually ten more), and was a prominent businessman. He was not a myth, but a real man who lived a real life.

Job is known as the man who persevered, and yes, Job did suffer a terrible and challenging test. This book gives us an excruciating view into the challenging trials that he encountered in his lifetime. But it also gives us a behind the scenes look at what might go on around us in the spirit realm. It shows us that the choice is ours to make about how we will decide to persevere when challenges come.

Job was taken to the depths of despair far deeper than any of us will ever be asked to go. He made it through by the grace of God and came forth as gold. That is why we are studying him as our second example. He endured and persevered through much of what we all go through when we feel tested by the Lord. We've all experienced a portion of what he experienced. Job felt the sting of death, grief, sickness, loss of position and stature, bad friends, isolation, loneliness, etc... He went through it all, and *all at once*! But here's the point, he *persevered* through it all and since he did, this gives us hope that we will too.

That should inspire some hope for all of us.

The History of Job

As far as who wrote the book of Job, we cannot be certain because the author is unknown. However, we do know that scholars agree the author of this book was an Israelite, because of the frequent use of the covenant name of God, which is *Yahweh*.

There are a few unique things that make this book one-of-a-kind. It contains the longest place in the Bible (four lengthy chapters) where God Himself speaks! It also contains the longest place where Satan speaks (two chapters). It contains more Hebrew words not found anywhere else in the Bible and Job is also filled with monologues and dialogues throughout it.

The story tells us Job came from the land of Uz. There is not a precise location of Uz to be found but in the book of Lamentations it indicates that it was in the land of Edom. This is east of what is now called Palestine and it is where Moses spent his 40 years in the desert.[1] The author of Lamentations mentions Uz;

> *"Rejoice and be glad, Daughter of Edom, you who live in the land of Uz."*
>
> Lamentations 4:21

Jeremiah speaks of places that will be in ruin and he mentions the kings of Uz along with other kingdoms.

> *"...and all the foreign people there; all the kings of Uz; all the kings of the Philistines."*
>
> Jeremiah 25:20

So Uz may not be around anymore, but just like Job, it did exist.

We know Job was a man of integrity, a man of wealth, and a man of spiritual sensitivity. It's hard to believe that such a man would live and that God would allow such traumatic trials to come down on such a good man. With that said, do you believe that God is acting unjustly? To read Job is not easy, but it is important for us to do so.

It can be a book of hope as we trust God and learn that we can patiently endure the storms of life. However, we have to choose first to trust Him during the storm.

Author, teacher and poet, Dr. Norman C. Habel said,

> "Preaching from Job is like nurturing a cactus garden. One is liable to recoil from the constant prickles and miss the blossoms in the night."

Job had Integrity

In order to get a better handle on the type of man Job was let's continue with the history first. Let's get some context by starting in Genesis 11:26. Here we learn that Abraham was the son of Terah. A few sentences later we learn one of Terah's sons dies (Haran, who was the father of Lot) in a land called Ur of the Chaldeans. Terah soon sets out with his family to leave Ur and head to Canaan but he only makes it as far as Harran (Gen. 11:28, 31). The Chaldeans history time-line is that their territory was east of the Euphrates and so is Harran. So that tells us they didn't travel that far.

Harran was a well-known center for trade and the Harran people worshipped the moon god, *Sin*. In Job 1:17, it mentions the Chaldeans also, so it is quite possible that Job and Abraham were contemporaries. If that were so, then the passage of scripture in Joshua gives us a glimpse of the spiritual climate Job was living in. Joshua's passage says,

> *"Long ago your forefathers, including Terah, the father of Abraham and Nahor, lived beyond the river and worshipped other gods."*
>
> Joshua 24:2

Job already shows his character and integrity in chapter 1, verse 1 by telling us *"he feared the Lord and shunned evil."* His reverence for God was expressed in his character and behavior; *"he was blameless and upright."*

This does not mean Job was sinless, but it does mean he was complete. In other words, he walked the walk and talked the talk and that makes him stand out when you realize what the spiritual state of his surroundings were. This should give us hope that we too can stand out in the integrity of who we are in Christ regardless of the spiritual climate we find ourselves surrounded by.

A while back, James Patterson & Peter Kim wrote a book called, "The Day America Told the Truth." It revealed the following poll results regarding what people would do if offered $10 million dollars. The results are surprising;

- 25% said they'd abandon their family
- 25% said they'd abandon their church
- 23% would become prostitutes for a week or more
- 16% would give up their American citizenship
- 16% would leave their spouse
- 10% would withhold testimony and let a murderer go free
- 7% would kill a stranger[2]

Now thankfully, the majority of those polled said they would not give in, even for $10 million dollars. However, the statistics are still surprising and frankly sad.

That poll was taken quite a few years ago, so knowing that our society has deteriorated much more since then, I'm sure those statistics would be much, much higher these days.

As far as people go, not much has changed from back when Job lived. Job himself was surrounded by people just like this that were willing to sell their integrity, too. Remember, Joshua revealed to us that he was surrounded by people worshiping other gods, so right here Job stands out because in his heart, he had determined he would not live that way. But like I said, that was the environment he was living in then.

Let me ask you something? You may not abandon your family today or even kill someone for $10 million dollars, but would you sell your integrity to save money on your taxes? How about to get ahead in your job?

What would you do about getting a better grade on a test in school? It's the same thing.

Those are good questions to ask ourselves from time to time. Being integral is in the little things as well. The things no one sees but only you and God know about.

It's good to double check. I know I want to be thought of by the Lord as a person of integrity. Don't you?

Job had Wealth

Job was also a man of great wealth. In those days, no one had a bank account, mutual funds, or stock market investments. Wealth was measured by possessions—which was mostly livestock and Job had an abundance of livestock!

Job 1:3 says he had, "7000 sheep, 3000 camels, 500 oxen, 500 donkeys" It's no wonder it mentions he had "a large number of servants" too—probably too many to count.

Commentator Alexander Pope once wrote about Job saying this:

> "We may see the small value God has for riches by the people he gives them to. Most of us can't even imagine the kind of wealth Job had. We really don't need to in order to understand the losses he's about to endure. If one man starts with a Bill Gates-size fortune and another starts with a work-a-day subsistence lifestyle, and both end up with nothing, they're still in the same boat."

Job as a spiritual leader

Job was a man of spiritual sensitivity. That seems obvious when you look at verses 1:3-5. This shows that Job was concerned about more than just his integrity; he was also concerned about his family.

> *"His sons used to take turns holding feasts in their homes and they would invite their three sisters to eat and drink with them. When a period of feasting had run its course, Job would send and have them purified. Early in the morning he would sacrifice a burnt offering for each of them, thinking, 'Perhaps my children have sinned and cursed God in their hearts.' This was Job's regular custom."*
>
> Job 1:4-5

Clearly, Job loved his children and wanted to protect them and keep them on the right path. He took seriously his role as the spiritual leader of his family. The success of that spiritual leadership is seen in the love his children had for each other. What good fruit he possessed in his life.

Some research conducted by the Christian Business Men's committee found the following: When the father is an active believer, there is a 75% likelihood that the children will also become active believers. But if only the mother is a believer, this likelihood is dramatically reduced to 15%![3]

Job appears to have been among those fathers who are active believers! It's obvious that Job was a really good man.

At his father's funeral, American Carl Lewis placed his 100-meter gold medal from the 1984 Olympics in his father's hands. 'Don't worry,' he told his surprised mother. 'I'll get another one.'

A year later, in the 100-meter final at the 1988 games, Lewis was competing against Canadian world-record holder Ben Johnson. Halfway through the race Johnson was five feet in front. Lewis was convinced he could catch him. But at 80 meters he was still five feet behind. 'It's over, Dad', Lewis thought. As Johnson crossed the finish, he stared back at Lewis and thrust his right arm in the air, index finger extended.

Lewis was exasperated. He had noticed Johnson's bulging muscles and yellow-tinged eyes, both indications of steroid use. 'I didn't have the medal, but I could still give to my father by acting with class and dignity.' Lewis said later. He shook Johnson's hand and left the track. But then came the announcement that Johnson had tested positive for anabolic steroids. He was stripped of his medal. The gold went to Lewis, a replacement for the medal he had given his father.[4]

The integrity of Carl Lewis' father was reflected in Carl Lewis' integrity.

I only bring this story up to set us up to see into the type of heart the man of Job was. Our lives can be good and we can be good people in them, but just because we are Christians does not mean we are immune to tests and trials of any kind because no one is.

It's all a matter of how we get through them.

Since Job is such a large book (42 chapters), we will break it down in easy to swallow chunks. I still encourage you to read the book through, there's a lot to learn from the dialogue exchanges.

Now that we have a little foundation laid for Job, let's continue on.

CHAPTER 1

THE TESTS AND TRIALS OF JOB

Reading assignment: Job Chapters 1 -2:10

With the book of Job, we have a tendency to only focus on just Job and his trials, but there was another kind of a trial going on in heaven as well. Scripture gives us a glimpse of the activity in heaven, a peek behind the curtain so to speak.

> *"One day the angels came to present themselves before the LORD, and Satan also came with them."*
>
> Job 1:6

Can you just picture this courtroom type of setting? Our Lord God, the Supreme Judge and Jesus, our Faithful Defender. Then, in walks the prosecutor, the snarling boastful accuser himself; Satan.

Here's the amplified version of this same verse that's more picturesque.

> *"Now there was a day when the sons of God (angels) came to present themselves before the Lord, and Satan (adversary, accuser) also came among them."*
>
> Job 1:6 (AMP)

What strikes me with this amplified version is it implies that this day was like any other day. The Sons of God were angelic hosts who were reporting to the Lord by coming before the divine throne. These ministering spirits had been away serving the Lord and they returned for further orders. Then in the midst of this normal gathering, Satan comes in with them.

If you recall, Satan was once one of the highest archangels, but he had been banished from heaven for his rebellion against God. Well, now he's back and God asks him "What are you doing here?" He answers that he's back,

> *"...from roaming through the earth and going back and forth in it."*
>
> Job 1:7

You see, this is the devil's main activity now—wreaking havoc on the earth. Peter tells us he's like a,

> *"...roaring lion looking for someone to devour."*
>
> 1 Peter 5:8

Remember, the devil is never idle and he is *always* on the prowl. These are a few scriptures describing who he really is and what he's really doing on earth when he roams it. John refers to him as the *The prince of this world* - (John 12:31)

He is definitely busy.

- He's Blinding minds - (2 Cor. 4:4)
- He's Stealing God's Word - (Matt. 13:19)
- He's Opposing God's work - (1 Thess. 2:18)
- He's Sowing tares (weeds) - (Matt. 13:37-40)
- He's Tempting God's people - (1 Cor. 7:5)
- He's Attacking God's Word - (Gen. 3:1)
- He's Spreading false doctrine - (1 Tim 1:3)
- He's Persecuting God's church - (Rev. 2:10)
- He's Deceiving the nations - (Rev. 16:14)

Satan Gives a Challenge

Now we find he is back in heaven with a cunning attitude and proposition for God. He wants to challenge God once again. Now remember, God is "all knowing" (Omnipotent) with all of His creations. He knows every tiny detail about everything He's ever created. God already knew Satan's underlying attitude and knew of all the evil he had been doing and had been instigating on the earth since he fell from heaven.

It would be good for us to be reminded that Satan is a *created being* by God also.

Get the idea out of your head of a "God vs. Satan" match. They are not, and never will be, on the same equal ground. All God has to do is snap His fingers and, *poof!* Satan will be gone—just like that. But God's ways are not our ways and His ways are not for us to understand all the time. It is not for us to ask why He doesn't get rid of him right now. But we do know that God has a plan for his demise and Satan knows the clock is ticking.

In the throne room, God allows Satan to speak and state his claim of why he's there. Satan begins his accusations and charges that Job's "godliness" is really evil. Satan goes on to explain that the very "godliness" in which God takes delight in Job is void of all integrity.

Think about it: that would be the worst claim of all if it were true! You see, Satan claims that Job's godliness is self-serving and he only *seems* righteous because it pays Job to be that way. He's talking about all of Job's blessings.

In other words: Job is only good or godly because he is being blessed by God. Satan suggests that if God will let Satan tempt Job by breaking the link between righteousness and blessing, he will expose the "righteous man" for the phony he is and the sinner that he really is!

Satan's Underlying Motive

Satan claims that if the godliness of a righteous man such as Job—in whom God delights—can be shown to be the worst of all sins, then there will be a chasm, a break, a hole of alienation that will stand between them that can *never* be bridged again once it is exposed. Even redemption would be an impossibility if this were true! So if this can be proved, then the godliest of men—will be shown to be the most ungodly.

Satan seems determined to prove to God that His whole enterprise in creation and redemption will be shown to be flawed, *radically* flawed! Then once exposed, God can only sweep it all away in awful judgment.[5]

But Satan is after one more thing. He wants to drive home one more point. Once the accusation has been made, it *cannot be removed*—not even by destroying the accuser! It would just be out there, lingering in the atmosphere forever, and that's what Satan really wants.

God, unaltered by this, accepts the challenge by pointing to Job who is a trusted and faithful servant of the Almighty. He knew Job would remain faithful to Him even if attacked by Satan. Remember, God is omnipotent, Satan is not. Job's involvement in this was not due to any personal sin of his own, but because God had already said "there is no one like him."

I always say God is about the heart and He is. Only God can see what we're all about even before we do. And God's opinion of Job was that,

> *"He was blameless and upright, a man who fears God and shuns evil."*
>
> Job 1:1

God knew Job's heart

Now let's remember again that God *created* Satan. Please let this point sink in because there is never a contest between them. They are not equals at all in any way, shape or form! God knew Satan's motive before he even entered into heaven to present his challenge. God knows all, God sees all, and God knows Job will not curse Him.

Sometimes God will use situations in our lives that end up ultimately bringing Him glory—even if it means being tempted by Satan himself. We don't know what is going on the heavenly realm around us, but God is trustworthy and He will get you through the challenges you face. It's just a matter of trust. God sees it all and God knows your heart. You just have to surrender it over to Him.

This puts a different perspective on things for us when we're being tested in life. It's quite possible that the Lord sees how good and righteous you are and knows you'll get through this. He's not out to hurt you. He's out to fine tune you for His glory!

We all lose our way from time to time, but that is why we need others to remind us and encourage us as we walk through our trials. You are not forgotten or forsaken! Don't trust what you feel, trust what you *know* is truth.

God Gives His Permission

God lets Satan have his way but Satan has to work within specific limits that God sets for him. We often think Satan has more freedom than he really does. Think of the time when you went to the zoo as a small child and you saw a lion for the first time. You saw the lion himself and might have been frightened but the adult who was with you saw the *fence* the lion was behind. It's the same way here. Remember the fence was a limit. So don't imagine Satan with more power than he deserves.

That's why God accepts Satan's challenge. He knows that by accepting it, God through Job will silence the great accuser.

Job is soon robbed of every sign of God's favor and has to defend himself to his friends over this being his fault somehow. He finds himself all alone in his agony. He knows in his heart that the godliness he carries is authentic and that someday this will be over and he will be vindicated. But the doubt from his wife and his friends bring a dark cloud upon him and oppress him.

> **God sees in us what we have yet to see in ourselves.**

As friends to people we know going through trials we have a responsibility as well. What we say to others can crush someone while carrying their heavy load. So follow what we learned through our study of James—be careful what comes out of your mouth.

This is one of the points being made for us to learn from the book of Job. It all gets down to the matter of the heart—God is always taking the temperature of our hearts in any and all situations we experience. What is the temperature of your heart toward God or a friend going through a long trial?

Sometimes trials and tests drive us closer to God instead of away. Satan's plan for destruction is thwarted by our love for God! God is love and love conquers all—every time!

God Believes In Us

Regardless of how big or small our trials may seem to us, God has faith in us and in our character, that we will make it through. This is why we are to praise Him for *all things*! He believes in us! And ultimately God gets the glory—like He should and deserves too.

> *"And we know [with great confidence] that God [who is deeply concerned about us] causes all things to work together [as a plan] for good for those who love God, to those who are called according to His plan and purpose."*
>
> Romans 8:28 (AMP)

Charles Spurgeon wrote:

> "It is no mean thing to be chosen of God. God's choice makes chosen men choice men… We are chosen not in the palace, but in the furnace."

Maybe some of our trials and tests are because we are chosen and hand-picked by God.

Job Suffers Great Loss

As we move on, we see that Job hears of all the losses of his 11,000 head of livestock—which is his wealth. I'm sure there was shock, but in his pause, he thought possessions can be re-accumulated again. However, the news of his children's death—well, there was no comparison.

> *"He got up and tore his robe and shaved his head. Then he fell to the ground in worship."*
>
> Job 1:20

Tearing his robes and shaving his head were signs of grief. Falling to the ground and worshipping doesn't mean he was happy over the news; it was a sign of submission to God.

> *"The Lord gave and the Lord has taken away; may the name of the LORD be praised."*
>
> Job 1:21

Job understood this one principle—everything belongs to God. *Everything.* The material pleasures, our money, our health, even the air we breathe and the lungs we breathe the air with—belong to God, and that even includes our children. They are His before they are ours.

Job understood that God has every right to choose when to give and when to take it back. God is sovereign and He is just. He is the Lord God Almighty.

If you have lost someone near and dear to you, let me first say I'm sorry. I truly am so sorry. That wound goes deep into our hearts. But I also want you to see that God may be mighty and just, and He is also a tender and loving Father. He will wipe away every tear you've shed. When you hurt, He hurts with you.

God does not have grandchildren.

Death wasn't part of the original plan. When sin entered our world, so did death. God understands your pain and hurts with you. Go to Him with it.

He is the Great Comforter and He will carry you through your grief. Invite Him into those places because you will never experience this sorrow on the other side of heaven. Let Him help you through this season you're in and help you find comfort in His love—and that can only happen through our worship of Him. His promise though, is to wipe away every tear and bring joy.

> *"Those who plant in tears will harvest with shouts of joy."*
> Psalm 126:5

> *"He will wipe away every tear from their eyes. There will be no more death or mourning or crying or pain, for the old order of things has passed away."*
> Revelation 21:4

Sometimes it's hard and painful to be a follower of Christ. Elisabeth Elliot wrote that,

> "To be a follower of the Crucified Christ means, sooner or later, a personal encounter with the cross."

Satan Tries Again

Job passed round one of the trials thrown at him when his response to the losses is to proclaim God as just. So Satan comes back for round two.

> *"A man will give up all he has for his own life. But stretch out your hand and strike [Job's] flesh and bones, and he will surely curse you to your face."*
>
> Job 2:4

In effect Satan is saying people might say they care about others, but first and foremost they care about themselves before anything else. Job might have been able to withstand attacks on his wealth and family, but he'll wither under a direct attack that inflicts personal physical pain.[6]

> "To be a follower of the Crucified Christ means, sooner or later, a personal encounter with the cross."
>
> ~Elisabeth Elliot

When there is personal and physical pain in our lives, do we run to God or run from Him? How do we respond? We have the power to overcome Satan.

Just remember what we learned from James and John;

> *"Resist the devil and he will flee from you."*
>
> James 4:7

> *"...greater is He that is in you, than he that is in the world."*
>
> 1 John 4:4

The Spirit of Christ that lives in you can withstand the enemy who is in the world. But first, we have to take an action step in order for us to get Satan to flee. I only quoted the last half of James 4:7, but the beginning of this verse gives us the instructions we really need. It says;

> *"Submit yourselves then to God. Resist the devil and he will flee from you."*
>
> James 4:7

The New Living Translation says it best, *"Humble yourselves to God..."* That's the key.

What is the posture of our heart when trials come upon us? Whether those trials are from our finances, our jobs, our children, our marriages, friends, or our families? Are we praising God or cursing Him? Are we allowing the trials to transform us into better people or are we totally focused on ourselves and what we *don't* have?

The posture of our heart is the key component of how we get through any kind of trial. Walking in submission to Christ and choosing to worship Him even in the face of adversity is a powerful weapon of warfare.

God doesn't hate you and you are not alone so don't believe that. However, God does want us to grow and change. Sometimes the only way to grow and change is through the pruning process. It can be an ugly and painful process but the results it yields can be spectacular!

As we'll see in the next chapter we also need to be discerning who we decide to choose to lean on during our trials. Do you have a good support group around you? Can you count on them in times of real trouble? These are good questions to begin to ask yourself as we begin to look deeper into Job's circle of friends.

> "Don't walk in front of me... I may not follow. Don't walk behind me... I may not lead. Walk beside me... just be my friend."
>
> ~Albert Camus

CHAPTER 2

ACCUSATIONS AND BAD ADVICE

Reading Assignment: Job Chapters 2:11 - 26:6

Please take note that this particular study chapter will cover 24 chapters in Job. I know that's a big chunk of reading, but it's worth the time to see the conversations that go back and forth between Job and his friends. You get a real sense of what is going on in their hearts when they speak. I encourage you to read these chapters because as you read you'll ask yourself—do I have friends like these in my life?

Martin Luther told a parable in which the devil was listening to his demons report on their progress in destroying the souls of men.

> One evil spirit said, "There was a company of Christians crossing the desert, and I loosed the lions upon them. Soon the sands of the desert were strewn with their mangled corpses."
>
> "But what good is that?" barked Satan. "The lions destroyed their bodies, but their souls were saved. It is the souls I am after."
>
> Then another unclean spirit gave his evil report about the same thing, but it was with a ship and the Christians died at sea.
>
> But Satan retorted, "What good is that? Their bodies were drowned in the sea, but their souls were saved. It is their souls I'm after."
>
> Then a third fallen angel stepped forward to give his fiendish

report; "For years I have been trying to cast one particular Christian into deep despair and depression. At last, I have succeeded." And with that report, the corridor of hell rang with shouts of triumph. The sinister mission had been accomplished. The soul of a believer had been defeated.[7]

This is the goal of Satan with Job—and a reminder that it's his goal to defeat our hope as well.

God, as we know, has allowed affliction to come upon Job. He is stricken with sores that covered the top of his head to the soles of his feet too. They were oozing and very painful. Your heart just aches for him! It's one thing to suffer the loss of all his children and be in emotional pain, but to add the physical pain too with open oozing sores all over your body is enough to break anyone!

Poor Job sat in ashes to find some sort of comfort for the oozing sores. And to add yet more pain now, his wife's inability to have any compassion or understanding was an additional emotional blow. Now he had lost her support too. It's hard enough in a marriage to have strife, but to have strife on top of pain is emotionally and physically exhausting. You can just hear her mock Job as she says,

> *"Are you still holding on to your integrity? Curse God and die!"*
>
> Job 2:9

I know sometimes we can say things we don't really mean. That is why it is important to think before we engage our mouths. Words really can hurt. However, Job had the right response to her;

> *"You are talking like a foolish woman. Shall we accept good from God, and not trouble?" In all this, Job did not sin in all he said."*
>
> Job 2:10

It's exhausting when others are insensitive with their words and you're in emotional and physical pain. Be kind and quiet when someone is hurting. Sometimes saying less carries more value than we know.

I remember when my mother was dying of cancer. I actually had a few "friends" who offered their unwarranted "advice" by telling me what I really needed to do with my mother.

"She should have done this experimental treatment instead of that…"

"Make her think only happy thoughts!"

Many of these same friends would avoid me and go the other way when saw me at church or the grocery store. They didn't want to really know how she was because cancer is ugly and they didn't want to be brought down. As if I didn't notice.

Trust me, the one in pain takes notice of who and how people act around them. They notice who is genuine and who is not. The senses become keenly aware of it. In hindsight you develop this sense and for the rest of your life you become aware of disingenuous people and that develops discernment—which is a good thing.

When someone is carrying a heavy painful load they don't need you to solve it for them (unless they ask) or to avoid them either. All they need is a gesture to show that you care at that moment. It's not about having all the answers. It's about being supportive and not being insensitive.

Job's friends started off this way, but then…

Job's Friends

Job's friends traveled quite some distance to see him. Remember, Job had lots of land so his friends didn't just pop over impulsively for a quick visit. It was quite a distance to travel for them so they had to be intentional to go to him. When they first arrived they did exactly what good friends should do for a hurting friend: they were quiet and supportive.

> *"When they saw him from a distance, they could hardly recognize him; they began to weep aloud, and they tore their robes and sprinkled dust on their heads. Then they sat on the ground with him for seven days and seven nights. No one said a word to him because they saw how great his suffering was."*
>
> Job 2:12-13

But then things began to change after seven days. They were left to their own thoughts which soon were their self-righteous thoughts. They just had to begin to speak up now.

> *"A good man brings good things out of the good stored up in his heart, and an evil man brings evil things out of the evil stored up in his heart. For the mouth speaks what the heart is full of."*
>
> Luke 6:45

So much for being a comfort to Job, because now here comes the poisonous darts from their pious mouths.

Judgments from others and self-righteous comments do have a stinging effect on us. They are like cuts that never have a chance to heal. Poison from such comments can linger for years and maybe even a life time. They bring division instead of resolution and there is never anything good that comes from it, because it is usually said out of ignorance.

Our Opinions

We live in a cause and effect world. We believe that prosperity and good health are the results of righteous living, and pain and loss are the results of sin.

That is simply not true and bad theology if you believe that. But this thinking is nothing new. Even when the disciples came upon a blind man, they asked Jesus who must have sinned? Was it the man or his parents? (John 9)

Sometimes life and the circumstances we find ourselves in are just plain hard. Life can be difficult and God in all His glory will use those hard times to refine us. However, we at times can be the responsible party for getting ourselves into those hard places from acts of sin. But even if we do, we should use it as a chance to humble ourselves, call for help, and reach out the One who can deliver us from it. In either case though, it is not our job to judge. That's the Holy Spirit's job to do the convicting so leave that to Him.

> "Satan is very clever; he knows exactly what bait to use for every place in which he fishes."
>
> ~A.W. Pink

My mom used to tell me that an opinion is meaningless unless it's asked for. If you decide on your own to weigh in on matters without being asked, then your words are just a lot of hot air. They didn't ask for it in the first place and you are the only one who has deemed your own opinion worth sharing!

Job's friends are like this. They decided that they indeed have something to say on the matter of Job's current circumstances and believe that he must have sinned or this wouldn't be happening at all.

The next twenty-four chapters are about them and their unwanted and unwarranted opinion and Job is left to defend his righteousness. When you read the banter going back and forth between them you'll begin to see the attitude of their hearts.

Let's remember that his friends weren't sent there to explain things. They were sent there to comfort him in his hour of need. If you are sent to comfort someone who is hurting, don't make it about you and what you think. Just be a good listener. The hurting friend just needs someone to talk through the pain with them. And some may choose not to talk to you at all. But just being there and being ready to serve them is enough. Remember, it's about them and not about you during this time.

An English publication once offered a prize for "The Best Definition of a Friend." Among the thousands of answers received were, "One who multiplies joys and divides grief" and, "One who understands our silence." Another read, "A volume of sympathy bound in cloth" and another, "A friend is like a watch which beats true for a time and never runs down." These were fine, but there was one definition that won the prize:

"A friend is the one who comes in when the whole world has gone out."[8]

Even though his three companions were the ones who came in when the world went out, they soon proved to be Job's problem. These guys pulled him down when they came around. His faith was doing fine until they arrived and opened their mouths.

> **A friend is the one who comes in when the whole world has gone out.**

Job had plenty of time to contemplate his life and his actions while sitting on the heap of ashes. And even then, he could not think of any disobedient act that would have brought on such suffering.

Poor Job was in pain both physically and emotionally and he began to cry out in his despair. So after a week of silence surrounded by these so-called friends, Job finally spoke up from what was going on in his thoughts in a flood of emotions that burst forth.

In his raw and desperate state, he curses the day he was born! When you find someone in a state like this they don't make sense. They are just all emotion and emotions don't have to make sense.

Don't feel the need to correct the claims made in such a moment. Most of the time, the person in despair needs a sympathetic ear, a meal, and some sleep. It is only then, after those basic needs are met, that clarity comes into the picture.

However, that didn't happen with Job's friends. During the next twenty chapters or so, there begins a claim and counter-claim discussion between Job and his friends. There is a theme between them of who's right and who's wrong and it doesn't vary throughout the chapters.

> It's been said there are two kinds of people in this world—those who brighten the room when they enter it, and those who brighten the room when they leave it.

I knew a doctor who called one of his colleagues "Dr. Sunshine" when he spoke about him. I asked him why? And he replied, "Because every time he'd leave a room, the sun would come *back* out!"

Let me ask you, what kind of friend are you? I encourage you to read the dialogue between Job and his friends. You may realize you have friends like this in your life or you may be like these friends. The exchange is quite telling of what kind of men they are.

With Friends Like These, Who Needs Enemies?

The three friends that were sent to Job were: Eliphaz, the Temanite; Bildad, the Shuhite; and Zophar, the Naamathite, and later another friend will stop by. Here's a little background and synopsis on the first three friends;

- **Eliphaz:** was the first of Job's friends to arrive. He was a Temanite, which means he was a citizen of Teman, a city of Edom. His name means, "God is gold" or "God dispenses judgment." He challenges Job that he is suffering because of his sin. Eliphaz tends to speak as a theologian, relying heavily upon his observation and his experience. He seems to be the most considerate of the three friends, but he still delivers stinging words by reasoning that only the wicked suffer. So, because Job is suffering, it must be because he has sinned.

- **Bildad:** was Job's second friend to speak. Bildad is a Shuite and he's from Keturah. His name means, "Son of contention." He speaks as one who relies upon tradition and history and he echoes the same message as Eliphaz except stronger: You *must* be sinning. You *must* be relying on your own successes and not God's. If you repent, then God will remove your suffering.

- **Zophar:** was the third to speak to Job. Scholars believe he is either from Edom or Arabia. His name means, "rough." Zophar speaks with even more intensity than the other two. He is a blunt moralist and he is dogmatic about it. Zophar is rude and curt in his manner. He is a pious and unbending man who points his finger directly at Job saying that he is *indeed* sinning and if he doesn't change his life here on earth it will be short-lived. It seems Zophar's concept of God is one who is merciless[9] because he was showing Job no mercy at all!

> "It is a sad fact that the tongues of professing Christians are often all too busy doing the devil's work."
>
> ~Donald Grey Barnhouse

I'm sure we have all known people just like these friends of Jobs. These types of people enjoy the sound of their own voice and have no grace for others—just joyless judgment.

Sometimes people just need us to listen and not talk, that's my point here. Listening is a skill that can be developed and refined. This is something that we need to work on constantly.

We also need to be discerning as friends to one another. Job's friends were so certain that their view of the circumstances was correct that they failed to see how blind and self-righteous they really were.

Let's remind ourselves what Jesus said to the Pharisee's (which Job's friends remind me of):

> *"You hypocrites, first take the plank out of your own eye, and then you will see clearly to remove the speck from your brother's eye."*
>
> Matthew 7:5

Job's view of God soon became worn down and distorted because he was so busy defending his integrity that he failed to see the bigger picture—which is God as the absolute reference point for righteousness and integrity. Instead, he let discouragement take over and despair was soon to follow.

Despair and Discouragement

> One day the devil decided to have a garage sale. Taking his finest tools of destruction—hatred, envy, jealousy, deceit, lust, lying, pride—he priced each one according to its value and placed them on the driveway. The most worn tool however, was placed separate from the others. A curious customer picked up this worn tool and asked why this one was priced higher than the others?
>
> The devil laughed and said, "That's the tool called 'discouragement.' It is more powerful than any other tool I have. When I use this tool on a person's heart I can pry it open and then use all of my other tools. It is my most strategic tool, therefore it comes at a higher price."[10]

Even though this is just a story, there is much truth here. Discouragement is the emotional state of being deprived of hope. When Satan pries open a person's heart to sow discouragement that person becomes easy prey for all of the other instruments.

> **"Despair is Satan's masterpiece."**
> ~John Trapp

Although Job responded well to his trials at first, his friends had become the devil's tool of discouragement and used this on Job's heart. The cunningness of Satan's plan was that this discouragement would stay under Job's spiritual radar, coming not from his enemies but from his friends.

Just recently I was dealing with this very thing. There were some pretty hefty tests I was walking through at the time and I didn't see that discouragement was overtaking me. It was under my radar, so my thought life and my perspective of it began to change and because of that, so did my speech. I found myself struggling and having a hard time coping with all of the challenges around me. I knew what God's Word said, but I couldn't make the thoughts in my head line up with what my heart knew as truth.

It took my daughter to sit me down and show me how I was acting and the things I had been saying. I had allowed discouragement to take over and despair to come in. That's why I was struggling with finding hope. I didn't know it right then, but I needed to be encouraged with kind and hopeful words that pulled me away from those dark thoughts and ultimately away from the people who were pulling down with them.

> "If Satan's arsenal of weapons were restricted to just using one, it would be discouragement."
> ~C.S. Lewis

Do you ever feel that way? This is an important point. Discouragement is a cunning tool the enemy uses. Stay the course with the facts of God's Word and don't ever just trust your feelings because they'll deceive you just like discouragement does.

A discouraged person loses all sense of perspective, choosing to believe the worst rather than the best. But here's some hard truth; at the center of a discouraged heart is also one of an ungrateful spirit—one that has lost sight of God's blessings and only focuses instead on the burdens.

It's important when going through trials that we keep our hearts filled with gratitude, even during the difficult days.

When Corrie ten Boom was in the Nazi prison camps, they had become infested with lice. Because of this the German soldiers would not go near them in their barracks. A Bible had been smuggled in and this allowed the prisoners to read God's Word without anyone bothering them. This brought hope in an otherwise hopeless situation and they were able to find that hope and hang on to God for a while without being disturbed. All because of the lice. So, Corrie gave thanks for the lice.

When life is hard and the storms of life are raging on it is important we hang on and develop a thankful heart. Christ is bigger than any situation so trusting Him with all our challenges only helps develop an attitude of trust in us—which becomes a behavior of obedience.

Remember, James encourages us to:

"Count it all joy, my brothers, when you meet trials of various kinds."
James 1:2

This is a perfect example of finding joy in the midst of difficult of trials.

Giving Encouragement

Being a friend who gives an encouraging word can turn the day around for someone. I have a few friends that I keep in what I call my *inner circle*. We encourage one another through cards, texts, and early morning phone calls.

Just this morning as I'm writing this chapter, I woke up disturbed because of a bad dream. I was in a trial and was at a low place in the journey. I was feeling a bit of despair coming on and could feel myself sinking lower. Not five minutes after I was talking to my husband about it I received a text from one of those friends who sent me some scripture to read that she had been using to pray over me that morning. It was exactly what I needed to turn around my thoughts and start my day right. God had used my girlfriend Joy to encourage me through His living Word and that gave me enough hope to pull me out of that slimy pit I found myself slipping into.

We may need help in this life taking our thoughts captive and fighting the good fight even in the midst of trials. I feel very fortunate to have a support system in place.

If you don't have any close friends or relatives in whom you trust, those little scripture books that have scripture you can look up when you're feeling a certain way are a great help too. Devotionals are also a wonderful way to be encouraged as well.

My point is that you can't fight all of this on your own. We need help and we need to be helpful and encouraging. Just be mindful of what and how we speak to others. Just think before you speak. Ask yourself, will this be encouraging or discouraging to them?

I heard a pastor once say when he lost his father, he invited Jesus into the moments of his great grief because he knew when he got to heaven he would not feel any of this. He invited Jesus into that moment to grieve with him. That is such a posture of love, surrender and vulnerability. It's the same when we're discouraged.

Invite Jesus into the moment. Focus on Him knowing it is only on this side of heaven that this saddens will ever happen. Let Him be there with you to hold you and to know He is hurting with you too.

It may not be for us to understand why we have to go through the trials and tests, but we should know and be comforted by the fact that He is there and He is listening and He cares very much for us too. As we focus on Him and allow our heart to be vulnerable, it becomes tender and in turn we become thankful and the burden of discouragement soon begins to lift. But first you have to surrender to Him.

> *"Cast your cares on the LORD and He will sustain you; He will never let the righteous be shaken."*
>
> Psalm 55:22

> *"Cast all your anxiety on Him because He cares for you."*
>
> 1 Peter 5:7

> *"Praise be to the Lord, to God our Savior, who daily bears our burdens."*
>
> Psalm 68:19

These are just a few suggested scriptures. Go to Him with what you're carrying and don't worry—He can handle it.

Job Still Stands Firm

Job and his friend's debate back and forth and back and forth. This debate continues up to Chapter 19. Toward the end of that chapter, even through his pain and sorrow, Job still stands firm on *Whose* he is and surrenders to what may come. He says,

> *"For I know that my Redeemer lives, and at the last He will stand upon the earth. And after my skin has been thus destroyed, yet in my flesh I shall see God, whom I shall see for myself, and my eyes shall behold, and not another."*
>
> Job 19:25-27

We have the benefit nowadays of knowing from the New Testament that Jesus came for all of us and that He is our Redeemer. We also have a better understanding than Job or his friends did of the war in the spirit realm raging on around us that we're all born into. Job didn't have the stories of Moses, Joshua, Joseph, or even Abraham's journeys and trials. That would have encouraged him! And yet, Job still understood in his own cognizance, who God is.

> "We're already in the presence of God. What's absent is our awareness."
> ~Richard Rohr

As we close out this chapter, take a moment and take inventory of your friends. Are they good friends? Would they be, or could they be, there for you if you needed them to be? If the answer is no, then begin to find some that will. We all need each other to point us to the way of Jesus.

Learn to be a good friend to others by just listening and make sure to invite Jesus into every aspect of your life—even the dark ones because He will meet you there, I promise you that.

CHAPTER 3

WISDOM COMES IN ALL AGES

Reading Assignment: Job Chapters 27 -37

> "We may see non-justice in God, which is mercy, but we never see injustice in God."
>
> ~R.C. Sproul

In these next 10 chapters (Job 27-37), Job starts to lament God's "unjust" treatment of him. Let's just say he loses focus. He had let despair, doubt, and discouragement in. Elihu, a fourth friend who had joined the other three, patiently sat quietly during all the many back and forth discussions. But he now speaks up and challenges the thoughts coming from Job. Elihu possessed the wisdom that had been missing from all the other discussions.

Before we begin the breakdown of these chapters, let's focus on God first and where He fits in all of this. In other words, let's re-adjust our perspective.

Getting Perspective

As we learned from earlier chapters, we know that Job was a righteous man. It is clear to all who read the account of his life that he was a man of integrity. But Job had been worn down by his friend's doubts and interrogation of him and some attitudes had begun to change. Job now began viewing himself as right because he knew he was a good and righteous man, and that everyone was wrong including God, and that none of this should be happening to him.

Job's problem though, was that he was judging his righteousness and integrity by an incorrect standard—his own standard. But God's standards for righteousness are Himself. He is the standard![11]

Job couldn't see that because he had lost focus. He began to see everything through his own eyes and not through God's eyes. Based on his relative standard, he believed he was righteous and was being punished unjustly. That's what happens when we look at life through our own lens. Everything becomes about us and we become "self" focused.

> *"As surely as the Lord lives, who has denied me justice, the Almighty, has made my life bitter."*
>
> Job 27:2

Commentator Steven J. Lawson said,

> "Job's trials really weren't about righteousness and judgment; they were really about teaching Job—and all who would subsequently read these accounts—that God is the ultimate Reference Point for all evaluations of good and bad, right and wrong, truth and error. If God chose to allow "Job-like" trials into every person's life, He would be right, and not just because we all deserve judgment; He would be right simply because He is God—He is The Standard."

Elihu states the obvious;

> *"So listen to me, you who have understanding. Far be it from God to do evil."*
>
> Job 34:10

God Is the Standard

Yes! Far be it from God indeed! It is impossible for the One who is *The Standard* to do anything but good. When going through our trials and tests we have to know and trust the character of God. He is not evil, He is a good Father. If we are going through something, we need to trust it's for a point that will bear fruit and benefit us later on.

Remember, Job's friends believed that Job was being punished because he must have sinned. Job assumed that because he had committed no sin—as far as he knew—he was blameless and therefore he was righteous. And if he was righteous then God was acting in an unrighteous manner and God needed to explain Himself to Job.

> God didn't earn His deity by being the smartest, the strongest or the most righteous. All those attributes are right and good because they are inherent aspects of God.

"I sign now my defense—let the Almighty answer me."

Job 31:35

Wow, what an attitude of pride here! It takes a lot of guts to speak to the Almighty that way. And to be honest, we often do the same thing. When we take on an attitude like this, we must realize it is rooted in a spirit of unbelief. What we are actually doing is thinking we are better and we have a better plan than God, which at its core is a spirit of *pride*.

Job and his friends had come to a point of only seeing life as black and white. It was a worldview of absolutes. Now absolutes are absolutely necessary for absolute principles. However, Job and his friends were misapplying those absolutes.[12]

Job's Own Snare

Soon Job became a captive of his own arrogant insistence that he himself was righteous. Eventually, when we reach a point like this, we are at a cross roads. It becomes a matter of the question do we want to be right or do you want to learn? One is unbending...and one yields to wisdom. God always leaves that choice to us because we are not puppets for Him to manipulate. We have a choice of seeking wisdom or picking foolishness by picking our way over His way. Which way do you choose?

If you find yourself frustrated with where you are in a particular trial you're going through, take heart because God has got this and He is building something great in you if you let Him. Surrender to His will and trust in His ways. He won't drop you. Just trust and humble yourself before Him.

The 19th century French speaker, J.M.L. Monsabre' said,

> "If God would concede me his omnipotence for twenty-four hours, you would see how many changes I would make in the world. But if he gave me His wisdom, too, I would leave things as they are."

Wisdom is seeing ourselves in any situation and applying God's truth accordingly. Having wisdom is essential if we are to take spiritual inventory of our lives. Truth requires knowledge which requires the application of that knowledge to be effective.[13]

> "God created the world out of nothing, and as long as we are nothing, He can make something out of us."
> ~Martin Luther

You see, it is one thing to know truth, but something else entirely to know how it applies to our lives. Knowledge is the understanding of truth; and wisdom is the proper application of it.

Job Lost Perspective

Job had lost his perspective of God's truth and sovereignty and became a captive of his own unbending stance of righteousness. He was unable to see that he could escape his torment by simply finding humility. Are you in torment over something? What is your stance toward God? Is humility there?

> "Humility is the most difficult of all virtues to achieve; nothing dies harder than the desire to think well of oneself."
> ~T. S. Eliot

Are we unbending in our need to be right? Or will we allow wisdom to come in and help us learn and flex a little. We're never too old to be taught this point.

There surrounding Job was one man who could not remain silent any longer. Elihu had listened in on the endless debate going on and he had had enough of what he was hearing.

At the famous Speaker's Corner in London's Hyde Park, a man denounced the Christian faith and issued this challenge: "If there is a God, I will give him five minutes to strike me dead!" Before the stunned crowd he took out his watch and waited. After five minutes, with no thunderbolt thrust down from heaven, he smiled and said, "My friends, this proves that there is not a God!"

In the crowd that day was a strong Christian who had the presence of mind to respond, "Do you think you could exhaust the patience of God in five minutes?"[14]

Elihu's Wisdom

Elihu had endured this lengthy dialogue between Job and the other men. He carried a mature wisdom with him that the other older men should have carried themselves. This should be of no surprise because his name means, "He is my God."

He was the youngest of the other three men and yet, he was the one who spoke with sound logic and had a correct perspective that the other three men were not using and did not have.[15]

You may be wondering why did he wait so long to speak? It was customary to defer to age first, so since he was the youngest, he was last to speak. Scripture does not tell us when he arrived, but clearly he'd been there long enough to hear the older men accusing Job of being a secret sinner and also hearing Job's self-righteous defense, too.

As Elihu was listening to the three apparently wiser men speak, he was becoming increasingly upset. He must have been ready to listen and learn from these older men, but found himself in sharp disagreement with their theology and their view of God. Elihu is now going to set them straight and defend God's honor. Just because someone is younger than us doesn't mean they don't have knowledge. Many young people are God honoring, some even from childhood. Age has nothing to do with it. Let's remember how Paul encouraged young Timothy by saying,

> *"Don't let anyone look down on you because you are young, but set an example for the believers in speech, in life, in love, in faith, and in purity."*
> 1 Timothy 4:12

Don't make the mistake of thinking that just because you're the adult or older by age that you are wiser because of it. The youth of today have more wisdom than we give them credit for. If we would just slow down a little, and stop and listen, we'd be pleasantly surprised. Many youth say this to me about the adults in their lives, "I know they hear me, but I don't think they are listening!"

Elihu made sure that Job and the older men really listened to him.

Elihu addresses Job

Job was longing to hear any audible word from God but to him, there was just silence. Using four separate speeches, Elihu argues that God had indeed been speaking but it was Job who wasn't listening!

Elihu tells Job that sometimes God speaks through dreams, suffering, and messengers. God had not left Himself without a witness. He was speaking, Job just wasn't listening.

> "God whispers to us in our pleasures, speaks in our consciences, but shouts in our pains."
>
> ~ C.S. Lewis

After Elihu said this to him, Job did not argue. His silence indicated that Elihu was correct. Each one of Elihu's four speeches was designed to correct Job's wrong view of God. Let's sum up the points Elihu made:

1. God is *not* silent (Ch. 33)
2. God is *not* unjust (Ch. 34)
3. God is *not* uncaring (Ch. 35)
4. God is *not* powerless (Ch. 36-37)

His arguments are truths that give us a balanced view of God and Job's view was clearly out of balance.

Elihu admits his anger toward Job and what he was hearing, but then he affirms that true understanding is found in God and that he was compelled to speak what he knows to be true! You see, it's OK to fight for God's justice, just do it with the right heart.

Let's expand on Elihu's points a little further;

1. God is not silent

Elihu speaks to Job using Job's own words.

> *"But you have said in my hearing—I heard the very words—'I am pure and without sin; I am clean and free from guilt.'"*
>
> Job 33:8-9

Now to be fair, Job never claimed to be sinless, so Elihu's quote is not verbatim, he's just repeating the substance of Job's argument, so this is a generalization. However, the point that Elihu is making to Job through his talk is that Job had developed a self-righteous attitude in his heart and that it needed to be called out.

Although Job had argued against his friends claim that he had "sins" of which he was being punished, he had overlooked the festering attitude that was developing in his own heart. Job needed a good dose of humility. Don't we all need a good dose of humility when we get a head of ourselves?

> "Nothing sets a person so much out of the devils reach as humility."
>
> ~Jonathan Edwards

Elihu goes on to say that God does speak to people in many ways. That He can speak through dreams and visions even despite the claims made by Job that God was being silent. God is always speaking. He is never silent.

> "We must sit before an open Bible and listen to God. What He says to us is infinitely more important than what we say to Him."
>
> ~Stephen J. Lawson

A teacher once asked his class what was the difference between listening and hearing? One student said, "Listening is *wanting* to hear."

Job needed to *want* to hear what God was saying to him.[16] Do we want to hear what God is saying to us when we're in the midst of a trial? Or do we just want to complain?

Reading the Bible, doing Bible studies, and journaling are just a few ways in which God will speak to you. These are disciplines that you can develop to learn to hear His voice. God wants to talk to you and He's waiting for you to listen to Him. Won't you slow down and try? We take time for everyone else, so shouldn't we make time for our Heavenly Father even more?

St. Augustine said, "When the Bible speaks, God speaks." The authority of scripture is the same authority as God Himself.

God speaks to our heart and our soul in scripture. We should remember that scripture is not to be debated, it is to be *obeyed*. It would do us good to also remember that scripture is sacred, and so be alert to what is being said. The true meaning of scripture is not to be gained through mystical experiences either. Let's be intelligent with God's Word. It is a cognitive message that requires clear thinking, rational thought, and intense study.

One last point I want to make regarding God not being silent. Remember that unconfessed sin clouds our ability to discern what God is saying through His Word. If we confess our sins then we are considered blameless before God. We are given the ability to see truths that are in scripture, so ask for God to show you your unrepented sin so you can clearly hear from the Lord and He can guide you the rest of the way through any test or trial you may be experiencing.

Remember, God is never silent. Scripture says that if you seek Him, you will find Him.

"You will seek me and find me when you seek me with all your heart."
Jeremiah 29:13

2. God is not unjust or uncaring

Elihu confronts the false assumptions held by Job and the three friends. He defends the justice of God and encourages Job to look to God with eyes of faith. He reminds Job that God is righteous and he must not seek to make God respond. This is excellent advice here! I pray we all find a friend like Elihu in our lives.

Voltaire, the famous French author and agnostic, once said, "God created man in his image, and man returned the favor." Like other agnostics and atheists, Voltaire believed that man is like a person looking in a mirror and then forming his thoughts about God based on what he sees of himself.

So, man's picture of God, according to Voltaire, was a reflection of himself. This is the pride of man!

This is exactly what happened to Job and his three friends. The counsel coming from Job's three other friends were skewed because it came from a false view of God. Only Elihu had an accurate view and because of that he gave wise counsel and he represented God correctly. Biblical counsel must be a starting point when advising and counseling others.

3. God is not powerless

The assumption of God being powerless is something that God will address when He speaks to Job directly. But let me ask you, how do you view God? Is He a punisher, ready to take us all out at a moment's notice? Is He mean and unjust? Does He burn with anger against us?

All of these views exist but are wrong views of God. These viewpoints actually started with the Greeks during the 1st century and the beginning of the Christian church. Before they came to know Christ as their Savior, they had been slaves to pagan gods and rituals. One of them was Zeus, "the god of the sky." He was known to use his thunderbolt to hurl down at those people who displeased or defied him—especially the liars and oath breakers.[16]

> **Don't measure God by human standards, measure yourself by God's standards.**

This is the Greek mythological god. However, we know people and even ourselves as viewing God this way. It's simply not true. Our Father in heaven is a loving God who desires a relationship with us and wants us to spend eternity with Him. We have to start there, or the foundation of how we think God sees us is distorted.

If that view is distorted then we will struggle to receive His great love. God really loves you with a deep and compassionate love and wants you to come to Him. He's not looking to take you out with His lighting bolt because He disapproves of you.

The first book I wrote was a companion study to the book of Revelation called, **A Revelation of Love**. The reason I wrote it was because I had discovered through my study that this is a love story to us from God. He will be literally moving heaven and earth to get us to come to Him and be saved because there is an ending of this present world that must take place before the New Jerusalem can be ushered in. Only God understands what true separation from Him means. He doesn't want that for us, not any of us. When I realized this, it changed my perspective of God and made me realize just how much He really does love us and wants none of us to perish! I *had* to write a book to share this revelation I found with others.

If you're struggling with the heaviness of going through a hard time, talk to your loving Father about it. But first, praise Him, thank Him, and humble yourself before Him. Your circumstances may not change right away, but your countenance will. God is big enough to handle what you're going through, so give it to Him. Now trust Him with it. He will work it out because He's bigger than your situation.

God is a good and loving Father.

As Elihu reminds Job that God is gracious and He is concerned with all of our affairs, that should remind us, too. God is faithful and sovereign and gives out justice without partiality.

Just like we need to do, Job was someone who needed to meditate on the divine greatness, sovereignty, and majesty of God. His divine greatness is mixed with His goodness. His divine sovereignty is mixed with His empathy. And His divine majesty is mixed with His mercy.[17]

4. God is Good

Elihu's wise words in chapter 34 are really center to his point for Job;

> *"Far be it from God to do evil, from the Almighty to do wrong. He repays everyone for what they have done; He brings on them what their conduct deserves. It is unthinkable that God would do wrong, that the Almighty would pervert justice. Who appointed Him over the earth? Who put Him in charge of the whole world? If it were His intention and He withdrew His spirit and breath, all humanity would perish together and mankind would return to the dust."*
>
> Job 34:10-15

Elihu affirms to Job the greatness and goodness of God, and God exercises His greatness for His own glory and for our own good. There may be painful experiences that we go through, but overriding it all is the goodness of God. Continuing with Elihu's last statement, even if we did turn to dust, God would still be good because He is the reference point for good.

If you can't see that in your life right now, then start with the basics. Start with a heart of thankfulness. Begin with thanking Him for the breath in your lungs, or the color in your sight, and thank Him for the knowledge of Jesus Christ and what He did for you. As you do this, your posture towards Him should begin to change. Dwell on His holiness and from this humble place, begin to make your requests known to Him. God *is* good and He is good *all* the time.

Who is God to you?

The most important thing about ourselves is who we believe God is. What we think of God is the mainspring from which our entire being flows.[18]

> "What comes into our minds when we think about God is the most important thing about us."
> ~A.W. Tozer

Just like the foundation of a house that supports the entire structure, your knowledge of God is what upholds your life and gives it direction, purpose, and strength. Who you believe God is impacts every area of your life—your attitudes, priorities, choices, and even your destiny. Trials and suffering can often distort a person's view of reality and cause him to fall into despair and hopelessness.

But we can affirm someone by reminding them of God's goodness just like Elihu did for Job. If you are constantly thinking that God is a big bad God, then how can you ever see Him as good?

We must go to the character of God. This verse is a popular one, but a powerful one too. It has always helped me find my way back to the right perspective of God's faithful promises to me.

> *"For I know the plans I have for you," says the Lord, "plans for good and not for evil, to give you a future and a hope."*
>
> Jeremiah 29:11

God Himself is being quoted here. He has plans, good plans for you and your future. Why then would He want to do evil on you? That just doesn't make sense.

In Psalm 23 it mentions that He leads us beside still waters and *restores our soul*. He's about restoration and healing, not beating us down. In the Gospel of John it says that God so loved the world (that's us), that He gave His only Son to die for us.

His character is about *love!*

When you are in doubt, search scriptures that encourage you about God's character. If we'll trust in His timing for what we're going through, He will lift us up from our trampled lives and restore us in greater abundance than what was lost during the time of suffering. It may be either in this life or in the life to come, but God keeps His promises! Therefore we (the righteous), must humble ourselves under God's mighty hand so that He can lift us up at the time He has determined.[19] It's a matter of trust and surrender.

As we endure our trials here on earth, we should be of good cheer because God will exalt us. That is a promise!

There is no subject more life-changing than God, and there is no greater decisive factor in how you live your life than your knowledge of who God really is.

Meditate on His great love for you and focus on His goodness. Listen for His voice because He is speaking to you. Dwell in the knowledge of *Whose* you are.

CHAPTER 4

WHEN GOD SPEAKS…

Reading Assignment: Job Chapters 38- 40

"Humility is the proper estimate of oneself."

~Charles Spurgeon

What a mess we make of things when we turn inward and only focus on ourselves rather than on God. Job had allowed his self-talk to take over and lose hope which made him doubt God. Job basically accuses God of being unfit to sit on His throne! The issue at stake was; could God judge with competency to rule the universe? Is God qualified to preside over all of creation? Job was so caught up in self-righteousness that he lost sight of who he was talking to. This is why it is vitally important that we take our thoughts captive.

Don't make the mistake of ever thinking that God isn't enough.

Never before had a Senate hearing drawn the attention that the Clarence Thomas judiciary hearing drew. Thomas was nominated to sit as justice on the highest court in the land, the Supreme Court. In October of 1991, unsubstantiated accusations were made against him. Thomas was undergoing an unparalleled character assassination. This attack threatened to ruin his life, his career, and prevent him from sitting on the high court. The issue was critical: did Thomas possess the personal character necessary to sit in judgment of others? Was he worthy to do so? [21]

He was guilty until proven innocent, which is backwards! Thomas eventually was cleared of all charges and did indeed get confirmed and now sits on the Supreme Court today.

But as you can see in the comparison, it was the same with Job. God had been charged with wrongdoing by Job, and must now defend His own glory and honor! He's guilty until proven innocent. Job, with his accusations, had lost the proper estimate of himself. You see, he had lost his humility.

> *"I sign now my defense—let the Almighty answer me."*
>
> Job 31:35

But, God doesn't take the witness stand like Job had set up at all. He turns the tables on Job. Job got what he wanted and got his day in court with God. But as soon as he realized he was getting what he thought he had wanted, he didn't want it anymore.

God suddenly bursts on the scene and speaks to Job through a storm and asks him over seventy questions. What follows is the longest conversation in the Bible in which God *Himself* speaks. The arrogance from the arguments was ruling the day, and God had had enough! He was tired of being misrepresented, so God broke His silence and spoke to Job in anger. He was direct, audible, and very powerful.

The Need for Humility

I'd like to caution us on how we enter into God's presence because He is God—the *Almighty*. Yes, He's our Abba Father, but He is the Creator of heaven and earth too. He is the Supreme Ruler. He is God.

It is important that we not argue with Him either. Isaiah 45:9 warns us not to.

> *"Woe to the one who quarrels with his Maker—*
> *An earthenware vessel among the vessels of earth!*
> *Will the clay say to the potter, 'What are you doing?'*
> *Or the thing you are making say, 'He has no hands'?*
>
> Isaiah 45:9 (NASB)

The word "woe" is a warning to us. It is important that we remember to be careful *not* to be casual with God. He is King of kings and worthy of all our praises to Him! We do not have permission to be impatient with Him by demanding an answer.

That posture with God is never a right thing to do, ever. It's with humility we approach Him. When we feel indifferent toward God, we must take a moment to pause and correct this before entering His presence. Job got impatient with God and he demanded an answer.

Pastor Bill Johnson once said, "Anytime impatience is present, often it is because we have a need for control." Think about that for a moment. When you strip it down to the bottom line of what he means, he's saying that needing to be in control is the absence of trust in God.

Simply put, Job lost his trust in God.

We do that sometimes, too, don't we? That should be a trigger for us to stop and pray and ask for help from Him right at that very moment. Finding our humility should be the first thing we do because it's the right thing to do.

This reminds me of the famous nursery rhyme written long ago;

> "A wise old owl lived in an oak
> The more he saw the less he spoke
> The less he spoke the more he heard.
> Why can't we all be like that wise old bird?"
>
> ~Anonymous

When God speaks

Please be sure to read everything God says—and how He says it—in these chapters. Let me help to give an overview and highlight some points. It's quite impressive when God breaks His silence in chapter 38:

> *"Then the LORD answered Job out of the storm."*
>
> Job 38:1

When God speaks it's big!

A long time ago, there was a commercial on TV about the brokerage firm of E.F. Hutton. Everybody and everything would stop what they were doing at the mention of the name of the firm emphasizing the importance of what they had to say. The voice-over would then say, "When E. F. Hutton speaks, people listen." It's the same with God. Except when God speaks it's out of a storm and everything that moves will take notice and listen!

He spoke to Moses out of a turbulent storm.

> *"On the morning of the third day there was thunder and lightning, with a thick cloud over the mountain, and a very loud trumpet blast. Everyone in the camp trembled."*
>
> Exodus 19:16

He also spoke to His prophets in a similar fashion;

> *"As I looked, behold, a storm wind was coming from the north, a great cloud with fire flashing forth continually and a bright light around it, and in its midst something like glowing metal in the midst of the fire."*
>
> Ezekiel 1:4

The Lord can be fierce and powerful, and yet gentle as a breeze as He was when He spoke to Elijah:

> *"He said, 'Go forth and stand on the mountain before the Lord.' And behold, the Lord was passing by! And a great and strong wind was rending the mountains and breaking in pieces the rocks before the Lord; but the Lord was not in the wind. And after the wind an earthquake, but the Lord was not in the earthquake. After the earthquake a fire, but the Lord was not in the fire; and after the fire a sound of a gentle blowing. When Elijah heard it, he wrapped his face in his mantle and went out and stood in the entrance of the cave.*
> *And behold, a voice came to him and said, "What are you doing here, Elijah?"*
>
> 1 Kings 19:1

God Responds to Job

God responds and humbles Job through a series of questions. One being,

"Who is this that obscures my plans with words without knowledge?"

Job 38:2

Let's put this in a nut shell, Job had been charging God about his inferior wisdom. He had charged God with wrongdoing. I'm sure you're thinking that you would never go that far! But you know what? We actually do when we develop an attitude toward God that's clouded in doubt and fear.

We end up accusing God of never being there for us. It's wrong theology and it doesn't line up with God's character. If we let our mouths go too far with our bad thoughts then we end up saying slanderous statements toward God's holy character. Job was speaking himself right down onto the brink of unbelief.

> "Who is this that obscures my plans with words without knowledge?"
> ~God

Hanging around the wrong people and thinking that we can challenge God rather than humble ourselves toward Him is traveling down a road that will only bring separation from God, and the root cause of it all is pride. When we're prideful we are thinking only of ourselves and no one else. This is what Job did. He went too far and God's response was to rebuke Job's right to accuse God of injustice. No one can take that stance with God, *no one*.

God begins by telling Job to,

"Brace yourself like a man."

Job 38:3.

I don't know about you, but if God tells you to brace yourself, that should be cause for great concern. If someone tells you to 'brace yourself like a man,' that usually means to prepare yourself for conflict! That's when you hear yourself gulp really big.

Then God begins a series of questions beginning with this one:

"Where were you when I laid the earth's foundation?"

Job 38:4

If Job did not create the world, what made him think he could run it?

Could Job explain how God suspended the earth in midair? What about explaining the sea, the sun, the clouds, lightning bolts, death, and the deep things of life?

God mockingly chides Job,

> *"Have you comprehended the vast expanses of the earth? Tell me, if you know all this."*
>
> Job 38:18

God continues,

> *"Do you know the laws of the heavens? Can you set up God's dominion over the earth?"*
>
> Job 38:33

The word "know" means to acknowledge or to make known. The Hebrew word for know (or "to know") is *yada*. We've heard it used today as "yada, yada, yada" ("I know, I know, I know"). It's used in the Old Testament close to 950 times! This means that it has importance.

But it is not as casual as we have made it out to be nowadays. It really means to declare as fact what is an intimately known reality. This is to acquire a deep and thorough knowledge of someone or something such as a husband would "know" his wife in a physically intimate relationship *("Adam knew [yada] his wife Eve." Genesis 4:1)*. Here it means to make a full disclosure of something about which a person has an intimate knowledge.[22]

God is making a point here with Job. He's asking: do you Job, have an *intimate* knowledge of when I laid the foundation of the earth? Job, do you have an *intimate* knowledge of the huge and vast expanses of the earth? What about the heavens above and the laws there, Job? Do you have an *intimate* knowledge of how I, God, rule over the earth?

It makes you feel quite small when God poses the questions the way He does, does it not? He did that on purpose because it should make us feel small. God is God and He does not have to answer to us about anything. Who are we to test God?

A college student went to class to take a final exam at the end of the semester. To his amazement he did not know the answer to any of the questions. Not one! He knew that he had no possibility of passing the exam, so he attempted to win his professor's favor with humor. Across the top of the exam page he wrote, "Only God knows the answer to these questions. Merry Christmas!"

He turned in the paper and went home for the Christmas break. During the holidays, the student received in the mail his exam that had been graded by the professor. At the top, it read in big red letters, "Then God gets 100%, and you get a zero. Happy New Year!"[23]

Just like that student, Job had flunked God's exam. He had not answered any of God's questions to him—not one. None of us would have fared any better either. Job was overwhelmed and was made painfully aware of his smallness.

It may be a good reminder for us as to how we look next to a mighty God. All of us need God's grace to stand with acceptance before His throne. But here's the good news, what we need God provides through His Son, Jesus Christ! Remember, it's not our place to ever challenge God. He is doing a great work in us as we are transforming into His image and that is a greater good. God's ways don't have to make sense to us. Check the heart and remove the pride that's there. We're nothing great *without* God.

Job's assumptions were derived from a false perspective about the positions of God and man. Forgotten by Job was the truth that God was the Creator and Job was the creation; not the other way around.

In the book of Nehemiah, the Israelites are back in Jerusalem from their exile and re-building the wall that was destroyed. The Law of Moses is discovered and read to the people out loud. Israel is finally in a right posture toward God. After hearing God's Word read to them, they immediately asked for forgiveness from their sins. Nehemiah's prayer to God should bring us to a posture of humility that we should take also.

> **The greatest injustice of all time was the death of God's Son, yet it was God's will because it produced the greatest good!**

"You alone are the Lord. You made the heavens, even the highest heavens, and all their starry host, the earth and all that is on it, the seas and all that is in them. You give life to everything, and the multitudes of heaven worship you."

Nehemiah 9:6

Only God created all there is and He alone gives life. The Lord is the Potter, we are His clay. He is the Shepherd, we are His sheep. He is the Master, we are His slaves. He is the Father, we are His children. We must never lose sight of the position of God as He reigns and rules. He can do anything He wishes because, well, He is God and He can! The psalmist confirms this,

> *"Our God is in heaven and does whatever He pleases."*
> Psalm 115:3 (HCSB)

Through this painful exam, God taught Job that He alone created everything. God created heaven and earth and all that there is. But even more than that, He alone controls all that He has created too. He is sovereign and not accountable to man—any man.

Finding Humility

Humility is the lesson revealed to Job by the Lord. Only in seeing and knowing God would Job find the relief for which he was searching. This is important for us as we live today. We are living in an age where man is relying on man and finding no room for God anymore. Our arrogance is showing through as we become more ignorant of spiritual truths.

As I wrote and prepared the book I wrote on Revelation, I found that man's arrogance is part of what to expect as the end times approach. The attitude of the day is "man is god." That's how the antichrist and false prophet will be able to deceive so many. People's eyes will not be on heavenly minded things so they won't seek God for guidance. Instead, when trouble comes their way, they will panic and follow men and their answers and that is a dangerous path.

> **God and His sovereignty is so immense, no corner of the universe escapes His attention or His care.**

Here's an excerpt from my book, *A Revelation of Love*, that the Lord gave me to help explain it further;

> "During the Tribulation, these are the two things the world will be hungry for, peace and stability. Instead of looking to

God for this, the world will look to government and its ruler. This false god promises freedom, but gives bondage instead. The Tribulation will bring hopelessness to many who will not recognize what we are actually living through. In those times, the world will look to a charismatic leader to restore hope and give direction."[24]

If we don't humble ourselves before God, we will be blinded of the hope that's in knowing God and be misled by evil—all because of our arrogance and self-centeredness. If you look at society today you can see we are closer than we think.

Job Can't Answer God

Job started off with arrogance which began to crumble away when he realized he had none of the answers to God's unrelenting questions. In fact, he didn't even know what questions to ask God! So why did God put Job through this painful "exam?" The answer is so He could reveal His greatness to Job. God taught Job that He alone created *everything*. But also, He controls all that He has created too.

> "We must yield our lives to the supremacy of God. How could we ever be impressed with our "greatness" after beholding God's true grandeur? The only proper response to God's infinite majesty is to bow before Him in total humility, giving Him priority in our lives."
>
> ~Stephen J. Lawson

Be aware of yourself and the language you use when you speak to the Almighty. Is it casual? It shouldn't be. He is not your pal, your bud, or your dude. This is your Creator. He is approachable yes, but He is the Sovereign King and Almighty God as well. Approach Him with reverence and respect.

God will never leave you or forsake you and that's a promise from Him.

"Be strong and courageous. Do not be afraid or terrified because of

them, for the Lord your God goes with you; he will never leave you nor forsake you."

Deuteronomy 31:6 (emphasis mine)

"Keep your lives free from the love of money and be content with what you have, because God has said, 'Never will I leave you; never will I forsake you.'"

Hebrews 13:5 (emphasis mine)

He will get you through your trials but you need to trust in His greatness and His goodness. He is working out something good through you so our job is to trust Him and to walk through it all by faith and not by our own sight. (2 Corinthians 5:7)

Be careful not to focus just on yourself. Remember, the only reason you breathe is because God has allowed the air to be here. Give Him the rightful place of reverence, glory, and worthiness in your heart. Start there. The more we humble ourselves before God, the more He will exalt us. It's all a matter of our posture and our attitude. What's yours?

CHAPTER 5

GOD FORGIVES AND GOD RESTORES

Reading Assignment: Job Chapters 40- 42

"The end of ourselves is the beginning of God."

~Carter Conlon

Have you ever been in a downtown in a city somewhere, where all of the big skyscrapers are, and stood in front of one of them and looked up all the way to the top? Remember how small and insignificant you felt at that moment as your eyes followed the building upward toward the sky? That must have been how Job was feeling after the series of questions God had asked him. His ego had been reduced to the size of a pea in the presence of a Holy God. God made sure that Job was made painfully aware of his smallness.

This exercise that Job endured allowed him to see God for Who He really was and he discovered God to be far greater than he could have ever imagined. It's safe to say he was awestruck by the magnitude of God's supremacy. This is a reminder for ourselves of the attitude we should have when standing before a Holy God.

However, God continues His questioning a little longer because He is driving home the point that God is the only One who can adorn Himself with splendor, glory, honor, and majesty. You see, God is God and Job is not, and neither are we.

Some feel God is being ugly and mean here. But that doesn't line up with

God's character. God just wants to make sure to be understood and use this time to teach Job a lesson. Remember, God's opinion of Job (when He spoke to Satan) was that,

> *"He was blameless and upright, a man who fears God and shuns evil."*
>
> Job 1:1

I don't believe God's opinion had changed, that's why being mean for means sake doesn't line up. He loves Job just like He loves us, but sometimes God will allow pain in our lives to transform us. Because like the Beth Moore quote I mentioned earlier says, "He loves you too much to leave you this way."

Paul reminds us in Romans 8:29 that we are being conformed to Christ's image always. It's an ongoing journey. Remember, our goal should not be getting to heaven, it should be becoming more Christ-like as we get there.

> *"In the pride of his face the wicked does not seek Him; all his thoughts are, 'There is no God.'"*
>
> Psalm 10:4

It is amazing to me to think about how people live their life without God at the center. It must be a very empty existence. It is God's mercy when He confronts us with our own pride just as He did with Job.

> *"Salvation, glory and power belong to our God."*
>
> Revelation 19:1

Job's trials were part of a larger picture which he and his friends could not see. That's why we have to not trust in what we see or what we feel, but in what we know scripture has taught us as *truth*.

Dying To Self

Remember what I said earlier, sometimes God allows the pain to transform us to be more like Jesus Christ, to die to ourselves. It's only when we "die to ourselves" and become humble do we bear fruit. That's the surrender I talked about.

When our daughter was in high school, she wrote on a poster board "I die daily" and put it on her wall as a reminder for how she is to live. She knew she was not in control of her life but if she would surrender herself to the One who is in control, then she would get through her trials that life was throwing at her just fine.

> **People can live their entire lives without acknowledging that there is a Supreme Being to whom they owe everything.**

Jesus reminds us of this concept of dying to ourselves;

> *"Truly, truly, I say to you, unless a grain of wheat falls into the earth and dies, it remains alone; but if it dies, it bears much fruit."*
>
> John 12:24

Just think of an apple tree. If the apple is not eaten, the tree will discard the apple from the branch and it will fall to the ground and die. But during that process, the seeds will be buried in the ground and in the next season, the ground will turn up a new apple tree that will eventually grow to maturity and bear much fruit on its own. Just like the apple tree, we have to die to ourselves first.

> **"Let God have your life; He can do more with it than you can."**
>
> ~D.L. Moody

God can do mighty things through you if you just let Him. But first, you have to surrender and die to your pride.

Job may still not have known why he had to suffer, but he now knows God on a much deeper level. Job confesses that before the suffering, he had a limited view of God. But Job has learned a great lesson through this trial.

> *"I know that You can do all things, and that no purpose of Yours can be thwarted."*
>
> Job 42:2

You see, Job realizes his protests were based on his ignorance. He says,

> *"I have uttered what I did not understand, things too wonderful for me, which I did not know."*
>
> Job 42:3

Part of our wisdom lies in the fact that we do not know everything. At some point we should be quiet and just trust Him. I have a plaque in my kitchen that my Aunt gave me. It reads, "God gave you two eyes, two ears and one mouth—which should tell you something." I wonder if I had known Job if he would have had that same plaque hanging in his kitchen after all of this was over.

Job goes on to say,

> *"I had only heard about you before, but now I have seen you with my own eyes. I take back everything I said, and I sit in dust and ashes to show my repentance."*
>
> Job 42:5-6 (NLT)

Remember, nothing had been restored to Job yet when he uttered these words. He was still covered with sores, homeless, owned nothing, and childless. None of that mattered any longer once he met God. He literally died to himself and surrendered to God in complete and total humility.

After the entire questioning, God lovingly extends His kindness to him. This reminds me of what James taught us;

> *"You have heard of the steadfastness of Job, and you have seen the purpose of the Lord, how the Lord is compassionate and merciful."*
>
> James 5:11

Doesn't that have a deeper meaning for you now? Regardless of what we are going through we cannot forget the character of God—that He is love. He is compassionate and merciful. It's about trusting in who He is and not in ourselves or the trials we are going through.

> **As we get closer to God we see more clearly our need to repent.**

Alexander Whyte was a great nineteenth-century Scottish Presbyterian preacher. Despite his great abilities, Whyte was profoundly aware of his humanity and its inherent evil. He saw himself more clearly than most men do. After one of his services a young woman came to him and said that she loved being in his presence because he was so saintly. Whyte was surprised; he thought for just a moment and then said, "Madam, if you could look into my soul, what you would see, would make you spit in my face."[25]

Before Job's face-to-face meeting with God, he probably would have accepted the woman's accolades had he been in Whyte's shoes. But after meeting with God his answer would have been much more like the one Whyte gave.

God Addresses Job's Friends

God's mercy begins by vindicating Job in front of his friends. The Lord addresses Eliphaz (probably because he was the oldest in the group and the first to speak),

> *"My anger burns against you and against your two friends, for you have not spoken of Me what is right, as my servant Job has."*
>
> Job 42:7

God takes a dim view of people such as Job's friends who might have destroyed Job—had he accepted their views. All of Job's friends had actions that reflected their beliefs. Think about it; they never offered to pray for Job or asked how they could help relieve his suffering. They just probed him in hopes to find his sins so then they could correct him. Know anyone like that?

John Piper, a prominent American pastor, makes the point that in this passage God is giving Job one more test. Job had said he repented but now we'll see if his actions reflect his repentant heart. He goes on to say as God tells the three friends that they were wrong in the way they viewed both Job and God, he tells them to take animals to Job and have him sacrifice the animals for them and pray for them. This is the way God required repentance in the Old Testament. Now Job could have refused to forgive his friends. I mean, they tormented him! But instead he does forgive them. He not only forgives them but also prays for them. He has passed the final test![26]

Isn't it like God to do this? Satan was allowed to bring him to the lowest point any human can go—physically, emotionally, and spiritually. But God shows Himself to Job and Job doesn't give up. Instead he experiences a deeper relationship with God and he chooses to obey Him because he has a truly repentant heart!

Remember what was truly at stake: Satan had claimed that Job only loved God because he was blessed by God. If Job cursed God and turned away from Him through the trials allowed, then the godliest of men—whom God delighted in—would be proven to be the most ungodly, the worst of all sinners!

If that were the case, then God's redemption for Job—and for all God's people—would be worthless. Satan would be right! So God uses man's free will in choosing God to prove Satan wrong.

God defeated Satan because God knew the true heart of Job. He knows that if a man's heart allows understanding and knowledge of God, I mean really know God, we (man) will always choose God over Satan and worship Him in glory and honor. The point of worship is the whole reason Satan fell from heaven in the first place! He thought, and still thinks, he is worthy of worship. That is the crux of the battle that rages around us in the spirit realm.

How awesome of God to show us His love and take us deeper with Him, so when we experience more of Him, we will freely choose Him and that choice ultimately defeats Satan at his own game simply because we are free to choose and free to love.

Next we see Job the servant become Job the intercessor, praying on behalf of his friends. Are we in a place to pray for those who have wronged us? Let me challenge you with that. Let's clear up something here; not everything Job's friends said about God was wrong. What was wrong was that they had misrepresented God to Job.

Remember, God was not punishing Job for his sins he was allowing him to be tested by Satan. It is never our place to judge someone else and their trials. You don't know what is behind them. However, it is our job to pray for them.

Job's Life is Restored

Following Job's forgiveness over his friends, Job's life was restored.

> "The LORD blessed the latter part of Job's life more than the former part."
>
> Job 42:12

Job gained more than he lost. He was prosperous once again and his livestock holdings were doubled! He had seven more sons and three more daughters—who were found to be more beautiful than anyone had seen before. That makes a total of twenty children if you count the ones already in heaven with the LORD. God had restored all that had been taken from Job.

> "After this, Job lived a hundred and forty years; he saw his children and their children to the fourth generation. And so Job died, an old man and full of years."
>
> Job 42:16-17

His life from that point on became more settled in who God was and focused on His attributes that make up His character, His might, His power, and His trustworthiness. There must have been an immense peace in Job to know his Creator this way and to never doubt Him again. There was no more doubt in thinking He isn't listening if God chose to be silent. Job probably was more sensitive to other hurting men than he was before, too.

> **We stand tallest when there is nowhere to look but up.**

Testing times have a way changing and growing us and heightening our emotional senses to others who are in need because of what we have been allowed to experience. That's why empathy holds more weight in a conversation with someone who's hurting than sympathy does.

I call it the three F's – "feel, felt, and found." I know how you *feel*, I've *felt* the same way, but here what I've *found* ... Empathy can be a great comforter to someone who is hurting.

Job now had a balanced view of God. It's been said that we stand tallest when there is nowhere to look but up.

J. Hudson Taylor, the founder of the China Inland Mission said, "I am a little servant of an illustrious master." Is this not the goal of every Christian's attitude?

James reminds us of this important point: Everything given to man is sent from God, and nothing is received that is not given by God. A few other reminders;

John said,

> *"A man can receive only what is given him from heaven."*
>
> John 3:27

Paul remarked,

> *"Not that we are competent in ourselves to claim anything for ourselves, but our competence comes from God."*
>
> 2 Corinthians 3:5

The secret to living life is understanding our weakness and helplessness. God's greatness and power

> *"…is made perfect in weakness."*
>
> 2 Corinthians 12:9

If we're to be used by God we must first understand that we're powerless before God. We have to surrender and trust Him. God could explain everything to us about His workings behind the scenes of our trials, but we wouldn't be able to understand it.

How can His infinite wisdom fit into our finite brains? All we need to know is that God is in control of our lives and that He loves us very much. So, if there is a trial you are going through, I urge you to stop squirming and look up. Look up and see the face of God and invite Him into your hurting heart.

Job's life was tragic at times and I'm sure there are friends and loved ones we all know who have gone through, or are currently going through, tragedies as well. Which begs the questions; how do we get through times of tragic testing and how do we help others who are?

It starts with relying on certain truths about our relationship with God. These truths begin with recognizing God as sovereign in all things—good or bad. God *is* God and He deserves all praise because He is our Sovereign Lord.

Second, we must accept His divine mysteries. He doesn't have to explain Himself to us or His actions. We just have to trust there is a greater good that will come of it.

> *"Oh, the depth of the riches both of the wisdom and knowledge of God! How unsearchable are His judgments and unfathomable His ways! For who has known the mind of the LORD, or who became His counselor?"*
>
> Romans 11:33-34

Third, take time and reflect on God's superiority. Charles Spurgeon once said, "The doorstep to the temple of wisdom is to acknowledge our own ignorance."

Next, we should refocus on God's intimacy. Are you growing in your knowledge of God? The only way to do that is to read His Word and study it. There are plenty of good podcasts out there if there isn't a Bible study available locally. Spend time in His Word and the Holy Spirit will comfort you, that's why it's called the Living Word.

And last, go to God with a humble heart and repent of all sins. King David was known as a man after God's own heart not because he never sinned but because when he sinned he was deeply broken over it and chose to turn back to God. Remember, God is a God of the heart. It was the same with Job. He was a righteous man and complete, but not sinless. However, once God revealed the sin in Job's life (his pride and rebellion), he was quick to repent. Job just lost his way for a while.

> **The doorstep to the temple of wisdom is to acknowledge our own ignorance.**

These are good examples that we can use to live by. My point is, it's all a matter of our heart. It's always a matter of the heart with God. Are you trusting God through your trials and tests that you might be going through?

The book of Job is about trusting God's ways above our own. Job is not primarily a book about suffering; it is a book about the sovereignty of God and our proper relationship to Him.

King David wrote this Psalm that is the perfect fit to our ending of our study of Job.

*"He brought me up out of the pit of destruction, out of the miry clay,
And He set my feet upon a rock making my footsteps firm. He put a new
song in my mouth, a song of praise to our God; Many will see and fear
And will trust in the Lord."*

Psalm 40:2-3

If Job were alive today, I believe he would have written a psalm just like this one. Celebrate the wonders of God and recognize He has it all under control. Surrender and die to yourself and trust the One who's got this, because He is a good, good Father and He wants to show you.

Go to Him now in prayer because He wants you to and He's waiting for you there.

The Books of 1 & 2 Thessalonians

Action Steps

PAUL'S CHALLENGES

What do we do when we come under persecution? What if we are wronged by even our own brothers and sisters in Christ? Paul teaches in these letters to the Thessalonians how to stand during times of persecution and how to be prepared in times of great stress and trials too.

Have you ever been or known a scout of any kind? They are trained in map reading, camping skills, and living off the land. They are trained with the help of a master trainer and a field guide to help them make good choices regardless of where they are, who they are with, or the circumstances they find themselves in. In short, they are trained to be prepared.

In these letters to the young church of Thessalonica, Paul writes a type of "field guide" for calling the community to service and there is an overarching reminder to be prepared.[1] Paul writes these letters to the church shortly after leaving them and being unable to return because he himself was being pursued and persecuted. He wanted to let the Thessalonians know that he was encouraged about their Christian faith and he wanted to remind them of his intense love for them. Because of persecution around them, he answers questions in these letters about Jesus' second coming and what death means for a Christian and how to stand in faith.

Some Historical Background

Thessalonica was founded in 315 B.C. by Cassander. He named the city after his wife, Thessalonike, who was the sister of Alexander the Great. It was a heavily populated and wealthy city that had a natural harbor.[2] Rome conquered it in 167 B.C. and transformed the city into the province's capital and the seat of the Roman governor. By the time Paul was there, Thessalonica was full of Greeks, Asians, Romans, and Jews all under Roman rule.[3] This was the perfect place for Paul to share the gospel.

Paul came to the region of Macedonia where Thessalonica was because he had had a vivid dream in which a Macedonian man pleaded, *"Come over to Macedonia and help us* (Acts 16:9)."

In Paul's time, Thessalonica had the potential to impact thousands of people from around the world because of its location and the fact that it inhabited around 200,000 people. This was an important place to be as the early church was getting started.

You may have heard the advice, "bloom where you are planted." Well, God planted Paul in Thessalonica for a short time and Paul used every moment to plant seeds by teaching, encouraging, and changing the hearts of others. Since the Roman Empire did not have a postal system, aides like Timothy took Paul's letters to the congregations there and then returned with news and answers from the brother's and sister's in Christ back to Paul. That's how they communicated with each other.

The birth of the Thessalonian church is recorded in the book of Acts;

> *"When Paul and his companions had passed through Amphipolis and Apollonia, they came to Thessalonica, where there was a Jewish synagogue. As was his custom, Paul went into the synagogue, and on three Sabbath days he reasoned with them from the Scriptures, explaining and proving that the Messiah had to suffer and rise from the dead. "This Jesus I am proclaiming to you is the Messiah," he said. Some of the Jews were persuaded and joined Paul and Silas, as did a large number of God-fearing Greeks and quite a few prominent women."*
>
> Acts 17:1-4

Facing Difficult Choices

The people that were persuaded to join Paul must have faced some difficult choices. They may have faced embarrassment from their families because of their "new" faith. Paul singles out each specific group and this would indicate that the faith that these people carried was strong. They handled themselves well despite the negativity surrounding their decision.

I remember when attending our church one morning, a young man who was a second-semester sophomore at Vanderbilt University, spoke to the congregation of his new-found faith as a Messianic Jew. He spoke of his love for Jesus and how he was shown the love of Christ and became a believer and follower of Him. He was sold out to his new-found faith!

But then he spoke of what it had cost him to make such a decision.

You see, he was an Israeli from the city of Jerusalem and he came from a strong Jewish family. He was on a scholarship to Vanderbilt University here in Nashville when he told his family about the exciting news of his love for Jesus Christ. His family responded to that news by excommunicating him. Now, I don't mean they just stopped talking to him, I mean they refused to recognize him as their son anymore and actually held a funeral for him in Jerusalem with immediate and extended family members!

He tried over and over to reach out, but they refused. He was dead to them now. He can never go back and see them because they won't accept him anymore. As he told his story he cried and the congregation cried with him. It was such a sobering moment of what a decision like that means and the cost it had. But even through that pain, he knew what the truth was for him and he knew he was to follow Jesus at any cost. Even if it meant losing his family. It was a high price, but one he was willing to pay.

What would we do? Would we give into pressure for the sake of tradition? Sometimes swimming against the current is hard, *really* hard. Can you imagine the faith it took during Paul's time to follow the teachings of Jesus? Just like the student I told you about, and the followers that Paul mentions, we know it can be hard to stand firm on our faith, but these are examples that *we can*.

Today we have the advantage of the New Testament for us to study and cross reference but not back then. The only way they had of knowing the truth was through hearing the Word preached by someone like Paul. They then made a decision right there that indeed what they heard was truth and they would then stand on it.

Paul's Challenges

When Paul traveled to share the gospel, he would go into cities and towns with Jewish synagogues. He chose the larger populated areas because he knew the good news would spread from there to surrounding regions. Remember, Paul was a Jerusalem-trained rabbi and that allowed him immediate access to the synagogue pulpits. When he spoke, his messages consisted of explaining, proving, and proclaiming Christ.

But you see, that came with a price too. Even though Paul had huge success with the gospel message in Thessalonica, it brought on hostility from envious and jealous Jews. Here's a taste of what Paul, and anyone who associated with him, went through when the Gospel message was being delivered:

> *"But other Jews were jealous; so they rounded up some bad characters from the marketplace, formed a mob and started a riot in the city. They rushed to Jason's house in search of Paul and Silas in order to bring them out to the crowd. But when they did not find them, they dragged Jason and some other believers before the city officials, shouting: "These men who have caused trouble all over the world have now come here, and Jason has welcomed them into his house. They are all defying Caesar's decrees, saying that there is another king, one called Jesus." When they heard this, the crowd and the city officials were thrown into turmoil. Then they made Jason and the others post bond and let them go."*
>
> Acts 17:5-9

This caused Paul to flee, but his leaving did not satisfy those angry Jews. They pursued Paul to Berea, forcing him to leave there as well! He was being hunted down and persecuted.

> *"But when the Jews in Thessalonica learned that Paul was preaching the word of God at Berea, some of them went there too, agitating the crowds and stirring them up. The believers immediately sent Paul to the coast, but Silas and Timothy stayed at Berea."*
>
> Acts 17:13-14

We need to remember whether living then or living now, the Gospel message will be met with hostility from the world. This doesn't change. Jesus said so.

"If the world hates you, keep in mind that it hated me first."

John 15:18

We must keep our eyes on Christ and what He may call us to walk through. It's not about you, it's always about Him. That's why in all of Paul's teachings, he drives home the point that all we do should be about Jesus.

Like the Thessalonians, we may face situations like these, too. As Christians today, we already encounter conditions that are at odds with those of the world. We each have faced some degree of persecution for our faith and we all live waiting for the Day of the Lord just like they did.

> **God shapes the events in our lives so that we can share His love with others.**

But as Christians who have been given the same Gospel message as those during the 1st century, are we mindful to share Christ with others who we encounter? Do we demonstrate Christ by our response to injustice, hatred, and oppression in the world we live in? Or do we fire off some smart-alecky comment in a face-to-face confrontation or on our social media outlets? God shapes the events in our lives so that we can share His love with others. It's important that we choose to respond to our circumstances in ways that our actions reflect the Good News of the Gospel.

If we're fretting and constantly worrying, that does not reflect trust in our Heavenly Father. If we're using bad and foul language, well, that's just obvious. How does that have any glory attached to it? It doesn't. The non-believing world may listen to what you're saying but let me assure you they are watching what you do more.

Do your actions line up with your mouth? In short, can a non-believing world tell the difference that you're a believer of Christ through your behavior? What about what you posts on social media? Is Christ glorified? He should be.

The Gospel Message

Paul touched many hearts with the power of the Gospel message. He shared the Good News with anyone he met, whether it was in a synagogue or in a casual meeting. Even though that was back then the power of the message has not changed for us living today. These letters that Paul penned to the Thessalonian church are filled with power and truth, and they are energized by the Holy Spirit. They are oh, so relevant for us living today!

As we study these letters to the Thessalonians just remember; they are like a field guide for Christian living. They're filled with practical advice for the practical parts of our lives that will help us live in an ever-growing hostile world.

I like to call them our "action steps" and I think you'll soon agree.

CHAPTER 1

FOLLOWING PAUL'S MODEL OF FAITH

Reading assignment: I Thessalonians Chapters 1:1-2:16

As I read this section of Thessalonians, my mind kept wondering back to our study of Job. Job was trying so hard to keep his faith even though he was being worn down by his friends. It's the same scenario here, too. The Thessalonians had found their freedom in their new-found faith, but the Jews and other non-believers were wearing them down by the persecutions and chasing Paul out of town. That was an attempt to weaken his ministry and hurt his reputation. Paul would share the gospel of Jesus Christ right in the center of the synagogues. That's like poking a bee hive! But truth was truth and it had to get out. Once they heard it, it was undeniable to turn from it.

Integrity was everything to these Thessalonians. They had to stand behind what they knew was true and what they heard was true. The attacks on them came daily, just like Job's friends, and it was beginning to wear down on the new Christians of Thessalonica. So Paul, knowing this, begins his letter to them with encouragement.

> *"We continually remember before our God and Father your work produced by faith, your labor prompted by love, and your endurance inspired by hope in our Lord Jesus Christ."*
>
> 1 Thessalonians 1:3

Why is it important that we remember our work, our labor and our endurance as Paul suggests? It's because we need the encouragement. Let's break this scripture down some.

Paul wants them to remember that our work is produced by faith. Without encouragement from anyone anywhere we would give up. Standing in faith for someone or a situation you've been praying for can be taxing on the hope that's trying to remain in your heart. That hope is battling with doubt and discouragement that's trying to take over.

We need friends in our lives to encourage us to keep on praying and not lose hope in the place God has us in. Just reaching out to let someone know you're thinking of them can inspire that person to keep going. Think of a missionary out on the mission field, or a parent standing in prayer for a wayward child. Just sending a note or taking the time to give them a positive word can keep them from feeling forgotten and inspire them to keep going. This fills the "faith tank" that we all have and need to keep full.

> "It is impossible to separate works from faith— yea, just as impossible as to separate burning and shining from fire."
>
> ~Martin Luther

Paul also mentions for us to labor in love and to hang on because our endurance is inspired by our hope in Jesus Christ. He's a real cheerleader for them to keep on going.

Having A Blessing Book

Keeping a blessing book can help to encourage us and to see God's faithfulness in our past and push us through the difficult times that we're in. It gives us the data to remember how God showed up and it changes our countenance to give Him glory and get our eyes off of ourselves as we tend to do when we're down and discouraged.

You may ask, what exactly is a blessing book? This is something I started doing back in the late 1980's. I started recording little blessings that would turn up in our lives. I just had to write them down and remember how God showed up. Here's how it started.

When we first got married, we were rubbing pennies together to make a living as musicians. Over a short period of time, someone had put money on our windshield, someone gave us a lawnmower, and our church paid our car note! I decided I should start recording these moments as Ebenezer stones for us to remember because God was moving in our lives and I didn't want to forget.

Another time was when our landlord came to us and wanted to get his house (our rental home at the time) off of his credit line. He knew we couldn't afford to buy it at that time but he loved how we took care of the home and wanted to give us the house. So he moved paperwork around to consolidate the rent we had paid over the time we had lived there as a down payment and suddenly, we were homeowners. There was no money exchanged at all! Not even at the closing. It was just a blessing from heaven and that's how we got our first home.

These are moments that are noteworthy. I would record these moments and date them. This was not a journal of thoughts—just data of facts to look over. Here's my point; when I look over how God showed up and blessed us it keeps me moving forward with hope during more troubling times. I knew Jesus was behind it all and I knew someday I would read over what I had recorded and it would help me get my eyes back on Him and off myself and the problems I was facing. It would renew my faith and chase the doubt away.

And it works.

I still keep a blessing book to this very day. It inspires me to keep moving forward. I'm on my third book right now and it has been an important tool that I use in my life because life has had many twists and turns to throw our way. We can forget all too easily how the Lord has brought us through the darkness. The Israelites experienced this too. The stories of how God had delivered them soon began to die out and it wasn't long—only one generation—before they had forgotten about the miracle at the Red Sea. It just became a "story."

Writing it down is a tribute to God's faithfulness from your past. It is there to encourage you when you're in a difficult time. God has not forgotten you and He never will. Don't let doubt and fear make you believe God won't come through for you and lose hope. Stories we have to tell are truly inspiring to us and to others! These are our testimonies of God's faithfulness. I highly suggest you begin a blessing book for yourself. Start today and write it down.

Faith and Trust

When Paul talks about faith, it is usually referring to a trust in Jesus Christ. You can't have faith without having trust first.

In our study of James, we learned that even the devil and his demons believe God exists and that Jesus Christ is His Son! But, the devil doesn't trust in Christ as his Lord and Savior.

> *"You believe that there is one God. Good! Even the demons believe that—and shudder."*
>
> James 2:19

Having a Christian faith goes far beyond our head knowledge of having a Christian truth; it involves a decision coupled with an action. Walking by faith and not by sight (2 Corinthians 5:7) takes a decision made from a place of trust and walking that out.

Do you believe God is big enough?

Faith and Love

The Thessalonians had a genuine love for Christ and they were living out their faith. These two things gave them the endurance and strength to labor hard on Christ's behalf. They gladly ministered to each other by doing things that gave them hope. Hope that believed God would do what He has promised.

True faith results in obedience to God that produces changes in our behavior.

The Thessalonians took *action*. They turned from their idols and false gods to serve the living God, and hoped for Christ's return in their lifetime. The news of their faith in God had spread and they were modeling an authenticity as followers of Jesus Christ!

But to be honest, they really couldn't have done this without it being modeled for them first, and Paul was the man who showed them what that kind of faith looked like.

If we break it down, we'll see that Paul modeled this for them in four ways;

- **Paul Was Willing to Take Risks**

Paul was an honest man and yet he was opposed, accused, and criticized. Going to Thessalonica was not a vacation. His work involved risk. The risk was in being there physically, not to mention the subject he spoke about and the impact that that had on others emotionally, too. People hadn't heard of this Good News before.

Paul also speaks of suffering in Philippi with Silas. They were beaten and arrested and spent the night in a Philippian jail. The next day they were released as though nothing had happened.

This incensed Paul! He pointed to his Roman citizenship. He was outraged that he was beaten and thrown in jail without a trial. This story is found in Acts 16:22-30.

Even though Paul felt the sting of injustice here, he still did not alter the message *"we dared to tell you the Gospel."* He did not buckle under social pressure, bad experiences, or other's opinions. This is why he's such a great example for us to follow. Paul did not just suck up his courage and march on, and God did not magically dissolve all fear or concern. Paul *knew* to stay the course with the Gospel message and the unwavering conviction of who Jesus is.

With God's enabling power, he knew he would be able to keep going and deliver the message of Christ. We should know that we can keep going because God is leading the way. And if He is leading the way, that helps with the risk of faith to follow Him like Paul did. Are we willing to take that risk?

- **Paul's Sharing Was Authentic**

He was not self-seeking and he had no hidden agenda. When he wrote these letters to the Thessalonians it was out of honest motives. They in turn, examined their own motives and observed their own actions. It was clear that their motives were indeed pure. They were not trying to con anyone.

Think about how impurity can destroy something. For example, drinking water cannot be labeled "safe" if one person out of 1,000 dies from drinking it. Truth cannot be right 98% of the time.[4]

Paul speaks about his and his Gospel sharing companion's, motives,

> "...we speak as those approved by God to be entrusted with the gospel. We are not trying to please people but God, who tests our hearts."
> 1 Thessalonians 2:4

The word "approve" is translated from the Greek work *dokimazo*. This is a word which is used in reference to metal purifying. It was a testing of metals to prove their genuineness. The implication is that Paul, Silas, and Timothy had the approval and commission of God because of the divine testing that they went through. God had stamped their lives as trustworthy because their faith had proved them genuine.[5]

The verse goes on to say they are not trying to please man, but God. Their entire focus was on pleasing God—and just God. Now, that is something for all of us to learn from.

Whatever you do, do it all for the glory of God.

In the early 1990's when President George Bush was in office, his chief of staff was a man named John Sununu. Sununu was once asked by a reporter if his job was difficult. He answered with a quick and deliberate "No." The reporter thought that Sununu had misunderstood the question, so he asked again, and got the same reply. The chief of staff explained, "I have only one constituent." He knew his job was to please the President and only the President.[6]

Paul and Silas knew their job was to please one person, and that was Jesus Christ. We could also use to train our thinking to make our decisions in life with an eternal perspective in mind and keep our hearts pure because God tests our hearts. He is always about the heart.

The Greek word translated for "test" is *dokimazo*. Sound familiar? It should. It's the same word used previously. It is a probing which is done with the full expectation that whatever is under scrutiny will be approved.[7] In 1 Corinthians Paul sums up what our commitment and heart attitude should be;

> *"Whatever you do, do it all for the glory of God."*
> 1 Corinthians 10:31

- **Paul's Sensitivity and Sincerity**

His love for others had driven him to share Christ's love. His ultimate motivation was love. To Paul, it seems love was a verb! He moved in the moment. He was a man of relationship.

To some, it seems easier to teach theology than to love the people you're speaking to. It seems easier to share lists with someone than to slow down and share your time with them. Paul not only gave the message of the gospel but lived an example of it, too. He was deliberate with his time and invested in his brothers and sisters in the Lord. He shared the joys of life and the headaches and heartaches that came with being in relationship with people.

In other words, He lived life with them, lots of life. Paul was a leader and he understood the concept of shepherding people. Shepherding is not just a job—it is a commitment to serving God through the people. When we walk through life with each other it requires a certain amount of sacrifice, commitment, and investment. Paul modeled what an effective pastor, leader, and friend should look like.

He was sensitive to the Thessalonians' needs and he responded to them with love. You don't have to be a pastor to love and serve people. Taking time to meet someone for coffee and just being a sounding board for them is serving Christ's flock. But here's my question; are we being deliberate in our investment to the relationships we have with others? Are we taking time to encourage and build each other up? Only you have the answer to that.

> *"Therefore encourage one another and build each other up, just as in fact you are doing."*
>
> 1 Thessalonians 5:11

Paul was passionate and sincere when sharing the gospel. If we're sincere and not phony, others will have a more open responsive attitude toward the Scriptures. This allows the conviction and truth of the Word to penetrate. Remember, it is not our job to judge or to make it our goal to win someone over to Christ. It is our job to be obedient to the Father. Just walk in obedience and let the Holy Spirit do the rest. Think of the parable of the sower and the seed. The soil must be tilled for the seed to plant itself firmly in the ground first. Sharing your life and being deliberate with others may help till their spiritual soil. God may not have you positioned to be the "seed-planter" for that person. You may just be the one who "tills the soil," so be obedient to what you've been called to be and do.

> *"For the appeal we make does not spring form error or impure motives, nor are we trying to trick you."*
>
> 1 Thessalonians 2:3

My husband came to know and accept Christ as his Savior in college. He had a friend who tried and tried to "win him to Christ" and it wasn't working. But what was working for him were his friends just being their goofy college selves and being open and honest with their love for Christ. They didn't change who they were.

By the time Steve heard the Gospel message at a church he visited, his heart was ready to receive the message because of the ground work that had been laid in him. He saw an example through his friends just being themselves and living out their Christian faith. Since his friends were just being themselves and not trying hard with an agenda for him, that canceled any preconceived idea of what a "Christian" is. What Steve witnessed was them just being themselves.

Can you imagine if everyone in his sphere of friends had an agenda to "win him over?" He would have run the other direction because he would have felt like a project. His friends had a sincerity that didn't judge him for not being a believer. They just accepted him as he was, and that softened his heart to being open to God's Word.

- **Paul's Life Was Worth Imitating**

Paul stayed close to the One we all seek to imitate, Jesus Christ. Paul's life was considered holy because he was constantly aware of God's presence. His holy life spoke louder than the words he preached and because of this, it drew people to him and ultimately to Christ.

We need to look to those who are mature in faith and farther along in their walk with Christ for us to learn from. Paul encourages the Thessalonians to imitate him.

"You became imitators of us and of the Lord."
1 Thessalonians 1:6

His advice is not based on arrogance but on the fact that he imitates Jesus Christ. Ask someone you trust to mentor you so you can be encouraged to grow. Iron sharpens iron and this is a great way to strengthen your walk.

Sadly, the media today, with its books and movies, have done a good job in tearing down the holiness of the position as a loving shepherd to people. There's a classic book called "Elmer Gantry" by Sinclair Lewis that is a perfect example. Gantry is a mercenary for the gospel—a holy man to everyone on the outside, when actually he's a con man. He manipulates emotions by sensational storytelling and yet, he is really uncompassionate and pompous. He has no depth as a person nor a heart for God's people. And although this is just a book turned movie, there're lots of real-life stories with personalities just like this in our churches today. I believe they are called "wolves in sheep's clothing."

A less scathing example—but still harmful—is the portrait of Father Mulchay in the classic TV show M*A*S*H. Yes, he was a quiet and kind man on base, but he was marginal as a holy man. He never managed to influence or persuade anyone when you look at it as a whole. The one that held influence was the outspoken and unconventional Hawkeye. Sadly, many of us view church today much like the character of Father Mulchay—church is nice, but unimportant. It's good, but disconnected from real life.[8]

The T.V. show M*A*S*H has been off the air for quite some time but if you look closely at today's shows and movies you'll see not much has changed. If we as Christians represent the church to the world, what are we saying in our message to it? Are our motives aligned with Gods?

In Review

So how do we follow Paul's example as a man of integrity and a servant-leader?

First, we have to be willing and mindful that we need to take a risk. We can't worry about our popularity or what others might say. Let's be mindful to use every opportunity to share His message in order to build Christ's church. That's what Paul did. You very well may be Christ's only mouth piece to that person you meet that day. Keep that in mind because it's so important to think about. Your life has purpose.

Always be yourself and be sincere. You don't have to have all the answers. You're sincerity goes farther than your Bible knowledge. Just relax and be who God made you to be. The rest will fall into place.

Second, always be sensitive to those around you. I'm not just talking about conversing with someone. I'm even talking about when you're driving on the highway, for example. How you act behind the wheel of a car can explain a lot about the shape your heart's in. And if you have a Jesus sticker on your car then really watch out! You're not incognito. You're sporting a billboard on that car saying you're a believer so what you do and how you do it is of the utmost importance at reflecting a Kingdom focused life. You have advertised that you are a proud representative for Christ so what you do affects *all* Christians. If you are blowing your horn because that woman is driving too slow in front of you, just take a moment and think. She may have a casserole in the back seat of her car that she's bringing to a friend who just lost her husband and she's driving carefully not to spill it. Honking your horn and waving your finger at her does not bode well for you and your represented faith.

These days our hurting world needs authenticity more than anything else.

Another example is if a person at work or at church is in a really bad mood. Don't immediately judge them. They may be dealing with a crumbling marriage, a prodigal child, or even a dying parent; and the thought of it is just overwhelming for them at that moment. It is not our job to judge, but to be loving and sensitive. There is often another hidden story as to why people act the way they do. There's usually a deeper layer under the one they are showing you.

When we share ourselves with others the way Paul modeled it has an eternal significance. What you do and how you act in your everyday life is serious work in the Kingdom and for the Kingdom of God. We are always doing eternal work. It's important that we take it seriously.

CHAPTER 2

PERSECUTIONS AND PRESSURES

Reading assignment: 1 Thessalonians Chapters 2:17-4:12

> *"You know that under pressure, your faith-life is forced into the open and shows its true colors."*
>
> James 1:3 (MSG)

Persecution

What happens when someone pressures you and or mocks you for being a Christian as you are trying to walk out your faith? What do you do? It's happening in our schools and to our youth over and over. When you hear the word "persecution," what comes to mind? Do you think of the early Christians being thrown into the lion's den? Or do you think of nineteenth-century missionaries being eaten by cannibals?

Is persecution to you something that happened long ago and far away? Persecution is happening in our present-day world today, right now. There are Christians throughout the world that must meet in secret to avoid being arrested. Pastors are being censored for speaking out on moral issues.

Terrorist groups are targeting Christians to kill. Christianity is under attack all around us and the attacks are increasing. Now we have social media outlets from which to claim our faith but then someone will literally assault you with hateful words on your wall because of what you posted. That also is persecution. It's all around us and it's not going to go away.

There is a comedian who is famous because of the platform he uses for the political issues of the day but also from making fun of Christians. He is a self-proclaimed atheist and has no use for God (his words, not mine). He's a highly intelligent man and well read but he loves to mock and marginalize Christianity.

He paints Christians as weak-willed and stupid. He had a show on cable for a while and I tried to watch it to just hear what he had to say, but it was so wounding to hear his audience members applaud as he tore down Christianity and its followers. It felt like the mob that yelled out to Pontius Pilate who wanted Jesus crucified. It's hateful, it's harmful, and it's gaining speed all over TV these days.

It seems all over the world and even in the United States, we're asked to tolerate everything *except* Christians and their beliefs. Persecution of Christians is heating up. This should not surprise us because scripture says;

> *"Everyone who wants to live a godly life in Christ Jesus will be persecuted."*
>
> 2 Timothy 3:12

Knowing this doesn't make it easy, but since we know it's not a matter of *if*, but a matter of *when* persecution comes to us, how will we react? Paul was concerned with this same question for the Thessalonians and if they would stand fast in their faith and against strong opposition. The same question is for us too. Will we stand in the face of opposition?

Paul as you recall, was in mortal danger if he went back to visit this young church in Thessalonica, so he didn't. He couldn't for his safety and for theirs. But how did Paul and the Thessalonians stay strong?

> **Many in the media claim Christianity is a religion for the ignorant.**

Paul's Persecution and Reaction

Paul was persecuted repeatedly. Jealous mobs stirred up dissension in Philippi, in Thessalonica, and Berea. Their source, of course, was Satan, and Paul knew it. He said,

> *"Satan stopped us."*
>
> 1 Thessalonians 2:18

and he voiced his concerns for them,

> *"...the tempter might have tempted you."*
>
> 1 Thessalonians 3:5

Paul's hope was that they would stand firmly on the truth; the truth of God's hope when they were tested through persecution. They had to know truth or they would be motivated by their feelings; and that is the tail wagging the dog.

Persecution and Strength

Don't let it defeat you. The persecution that the Thessalonians received came as no surprise to them because they saw Paul suffer and had heard about the churches under the same type persecution in Judea.

Persecution comes to us all in many ways, shapes, and forms. We don't escape it just because we're believers. Christians from all over the world are being persecuted today. Get around other believers to help you stand strong under the persecution you may find yourself going through. Have hope because God encourages us with His promises that He will sustain us in troubled times.

There are so many promises God makes in His Word about this. These are just some to keep on our minds:

> *"God is just: He will pay back trouble to those who trouble you."*
>
> 2 Thessalonians 1:6

> *"For in the day of trouble He will keep me safe in His dwelling; He will hide me in the shelter of His sacred tent and set me high upon a rock."*
>
> Psalm 27:5

God is the ultimate judge of those who persecute us and He is there with us, covering us. I encourage you to look up any scriptures that deal with God's promises and God's protection. They are there to remind us to stand firm in our faith because this is not our home. And knowing this should inspire us to keep going.

The Thessalonians demonstrated all the marks of a transformed life: faith, love, and hope. Their faith inspired them to turn and work for God. Their labor was prompted by love and their endurance was inspired by their hope in Jesus and His promised return. They believed in truth.

It's about truth based on trust. When we trust God's Word and what it says, we accept it into the depths of our hearts and minds. This gives us the desire and power to live it out and therefore share it. It really is about dying to ourselves and trusting in what God has for us. So be awake to opportunities God gives you to share His message. Just be yourself and be sincere. You don't have to have all the answers right now.

> "Christian truth must not only be believed, it must be obeyed. Men must do the truth."
>
> ~John A. Mackay

Just trust the Holy Spirit for that because He does! Let Him do the rest.

God's Sovereignty

The sovereignty of God ultimately gives permission for persecution. But we can be assured that He can use persecution as an effective tool to deepen our faith and commitment. You may be challenged by that, but it's about knowing and trusting in God's character. If we think about it, it's really never about us anyway; it's always about God. We need to surrender and trust Him in all things.

> *"Trust in the Lord with* all *your heart, lean not on your own understanding. In* all *your ways acknowledge Him, and He will make your paths straight."*
>
> Proverbs 3:5-6 (emphasis mine)

Don't try to figure this out yourself. We don't have to understand God's ways all the time, we just have to keep seeking Him and He will bring us through the trials.

It's also important to remember that God will not allow more testing than we can bear.

> *"No temptation has overtaken you except what is common to mankind. And God is faithful; He will not let you be tempted beyond what you can bear. But when you are tempted, He will also provide a way out so that you can endure it."*
>
> 1 Corinthians 10:13

Satan has limited power to what God will allow. Remember Job? However, if we allow ourselves to be discouraged about the trials we face, we might abandon our faith all together. It was this kind of discouragement that Paul was afraid of for the Thessalonians. But you see, the key is not if and how we're tested, but our *response* to it.

Do you ever worry? This is our human tendency that arises from our inability to know what the future holds. It stems from our limited knowledge and experience—and at times our faith.

When We're Anxious

Paul is the same person who wrote;

> *"Do not be anxious about anything…"*
>
> Philippians 4:6

and then he writes to the Thessalonians;

> *"When I could stand it no longer…I was afraid."*
>
> 1 Thessalonians 3:5

Is there a contradiction here? He sounds a bit anxious.

There are two different kinds of worry or anxiety.

- One is worrying or fretting over situations we cannot control or influence.
- The other concerns real dangers or possibilities.[9]

Paul's anxiety grew out of the second type because of the young faith that the Thessalonians had. He was worried and feeling anxious that they would fall away. We all feel that sometimes with our friends whose faith is young in the Lord. So how do we battle that? We battle that by *prayer*. Prayer is a powerful tool in the fight of faith.

In the same way, Paul knew that sitting around worrying would not solve anything and would be counterproductive. Worry without action—however it may be justified—ruins our health, our well-being, and offers no solution either. So Paul prayed. He understood that prayer is not an empty exercise. It is the power of God brought to bear upon a dilemma.[10] Here is the complete passage from Paul:

> *"Do not be anxious about anything, but in everything, by prayer and petition, with thanksgiving, present your requests to God."*
>
> Philippians 4:6

If we continue to be anxious then we are overcome with worry. And according to Oswald Chambers, worrying results in sinning. We tend to think that worrying is helping the problem to get solved. But what's really happening is that we are elevating ourselves over God. We are trying to take control and are not releasing it to Him like we are told to do. God doesn't need our help. When you worry, you're making plans without God.[11]

Prayer and Petition

If you find yourself in a difficult time right now and you are slipping away into a place of despair and are struggling to pray, release it to the Lord. Then find another Christian brother or sister who will stand with you in prayer and encourage you. They can be that person who will stand in that place for you when you can't at that moment.

> "I'll lean on you and you'll lean on me and we'll be OK."
>
> ~Dave Matthews

I never want to downplay the challenges of life. It's a struggle to not be anxious when we need help. Lean on the ones who will stand with you.

When you become physically sick what do you do? You rest so your body can heal. It's the same with our spiritual lives. Once you come close to despair, God's message in scripture is not always, *"Be strong and courageous!"* (Joshua 1:6) for He knows that your strength and courage have run away. Instead, sometimes God wants to sweetly remind you to, *"Be still and know that I am God."* (Psalm 46:10)

That is all God asks of you. He will sustain you and bring you through the fire.[11] Sometimes He sends good friends for you to lean on who are willing to stand in your place and pray for you. We're not meant to walk through this life alone. We go through life together.

The Importance of Words

Why are words important? Why is knowing scripture important? Commentator Knute Larson gives a great explanation on this:

"Most of us are acquainted with the playground rhyme, 'Sticks and stones may break my bones, but words will never hurt me.' This is patently wrong. Words do have power. Bruises and broken bones will heal, but words sink deep within our minds and souls. We carry their joy or poison with us wherever we go, and they can affect us for a lifetime. They can heal or wound, inspire or devastate. Perhaps that is why Jesus warned that,

> *"Men will have to give account of the Day of Judgment for every careless word they have spoken. For by your words you will be acquitted, and by your words you will be condemned."*
>
> Matthew 12:36-37

Jesus says this because

> *"out of the overflow of the heart the mouth speaks."*
>
> Matthew 12:34

"If our words hold that kind of power, carrying our hearts upon their breath, what about God's words then? God's words revealed the overflow of His heart:

> *"The word of the Lord is flawless."*
>
> 2 Samuel 22:31

"God is perfect, complete, the source of all truth and reality. His Word carries the dynamic part of His nature and it speaks with the power of an eternal reality. That is why He could speak the world into existence."[12]

Mr. Larson goes on to say; "God's Word has inherent power because it is the carrier of undisputed truth. Nothing can withstand it, succeed against it, overcome it, or disprove its truth. In fact, God's Word,

> "...is living and active. Sharper than any double-edged sword, it penetrates even to dividing soul and spirit, joints and marrow, it judges the thoughts and attitudes of the heart."
>
> Hebrews 4:12

God's Word is timeless and yet present. These are not just ideas we read and study about in the Bible, they are the contemporary thoughts and expressions of the boundless God who is always now and always present. That's why they are living words used by the Holy Spirit to penetrate and effect change where mere words or ideas could not. But it is also important to note that it takes faith to work with these powerful and truthful words so that they then affect change. James would agree because he writes,

> "Do not merely listen to the Word, and so deceive yourselves. Do what it says."
>
> James 1:22

The Word of God, the Bible, is more than an interesting book to study. It is more than good ideas, beautiful prose, or poetry. It is not to be trivialized, ignored, or mishandled because if we do, we could be in danger of God's wrath. This should cause us to take seriously the words of God which are revealed by His mercy to us who are dependent upon His grace."[13]

> "A positive attitude causes a chain reaction of positive thoughts, events and outcomes. It is a catalyst and sparks extraordinary results."
> ~Wade Boggs

The Thessalonians recognized His mercy, His grace, and the implication of hearing what God was really saying. We need to recapture that same awe and reverence that comes from being given the thoughts of our eternal God. Just ask Him for help to do so and He will.

Keeping a Good Attitude

Paul wanted to go back and see the Thessalonians but couldn't and I'm sure that was a point of sadness for him. However, he was overjoyed when he found out his prayers for their growth and love were being answered. Receiving this information was important because Paul was relying on three key things to keep him going.

First, he kept a good attitude in the face of adversity. He didn't complain or worry but continued to persevere in his faith with a joyful heart, even though he was being unfairly persecuted.

You might be asking yourself then, how can joy and persecution co-exist? Paul explains;

> *"But Timothy has just now come to us from you and has brought good news about your faith and love. He has told us that you always have pleasant memories of us and that you long to see us, just as we also long to see you. Therefore, brothers and sisters, in all our distress and persecution we were encouraged about you because of your faith. For now we really live, since you are standing firm in the Lord. How can we thank God enough for you in return for all the joy we have in the presence of our God because of you?"*
>
> 1 Thessalonians 3:6-9

We can all benefit when someone brings a word of encouragement because a little bit goes a long way. If you want to tell someone how much what they said to you, or the card they sent, or the hug they gave, meant to you, tell the person! That encouragement will help them as much as their word or action helped you. The point is, don't just think it—do it.

Second, Paul is thrilled that they remembered him fondly rather than dwelling on the ugly lies that jealous men were spreading. He doesn't ignore the distress and persecution but he doesn't fall into complaining about it either. He doesn't partner with bad thoughts like fear and doubt. When we take on those thoughts, we are partnering with the darkness from which they originated. Paul's good attitude is further bolstered by prayer and he prays with a spirit of thanksgiving and joy.

Paul prays continuously and longs to complete the job the Lord has given him. This is a discipline that we can develop, too, but it first starts with understanding God's character and that is one of love. He is a loving Father so give Him thanks first, then watch over your mouth to not give voice to the poisonous thoughts that may come.

> "Whoever controls the media, controls the mind."
> ~Jim Morrison

It can work the other way around too. It is important to be around like-minded and Godly people that can keep you uplifted and heavenly minded as you walk through your trials. Also be guarded on your choices of entertainment.

Make sure they are not the cause of your dark moods and depressions because this can affect what lens you view the world with. Is it one of hope or despair?

And third, Paul loved lavishly! Paul was able to love in such a big way because he understood God's love. We should love each other lavishly too. It is not possible for us to love wholly or unselfishly without relying on God to love others through us.

Reacting To Our Circumstances

Our circumstances don't matter as much as how we react to them. How do you react in the face of adversity? Think of a time when you faced great trials. Maybe you're going through one now. Paul's example shows us we should count our blessings, pray earnestly, and love lavishly! But to do so we must rely on the Holy Spirit to be present in us every hour of every day to help us maintain our faith with a joyful heart.

Here's a personal example I want to share with you;

One Saturday I was going to meet a friend for lunch north of town. Afterwards, I was to come home and pick up my husband and then go see some friends we hadn't seen in a while. We were going to have dinner at their house which was on the east side of town. We live on the south side of town so I knew I was going to be all over the place that day. Because I was also getting to see some old friends that I hadn't seen in quite a while, I didn't mind the full day of driving everywhere. I knew it would be a fulfilling day for my heart.

Two things to know: First, Nashville (where we live) has three interstates running through it. There are several parts that you navigate carefully because of the merges involved and the speeds that everyone drives. Second, we had been having some problems with our van. Since they were intermittent and things were okay at that moment, I jumped in the van and took off.

As soon as I hit the interstate the van shakes and the engine light comes on. *Argh!* But I wasn't going to let that get me down so I immediately turned around and headed back home. I called my husband and just said, "I'm taking your car. I'll only be a little late to see my friend Donna and we'll take the van in on Monday."

I parked the van back in the driveway and took Steve's car. Steve's car is... well... let's just say we don't take it out on the highway much because it's on a wing and a prayer.

Oh, one more thing, Donna, the friend I was meeting for lunch, doesn't like cell phones, so I couldn't call her. As I got to the center of Nashville, where two of the interstates merge, Steve's car died because of the stop-and-go traffic. I could not get it to start. All it did was cough and sputter and cough—right in the middle of traffic. Another *Argh!*

Thankfully I was able to coast down a slight incline onto the shoulder at the corner of one of the merges. I took a breath—determined to keep a good attitude—and called my husband. But remember, all he had was the intermittent van.

Also remember that I can't reach my girlfriend to tell her I can't come now because she doesn't have a cell phone. So, there I sit in the hot, humid sun (oh yeah, I forgot to mention—it was in the middle of July!) with my makeup melting off my face.

People are driving by, honking and yelling as if it is my fault—as if I wanted to be there on the shoulder, broken down. But I didn't let that sway my spirits! I found the restaurant's phone number through my cell phone, had Donna paged, and eventually reached her. She was disappointed but I kept things positive for her. My husband called a friend, Travis, who owns a wrecker service. He didn't have his truck with him that Saturday afternoon but he was near me and would come to see if he could help. As I waited for Travis to come, I called our friends who we were going to have dinner with that evening.

Since we didn't have a working car that could be trusted, I had to cancel our plans. Cindi was disappointed because we had had this on our calendar for months but I kept a good attitude and counted the blessings with her. She prayed for me and that was helpful and encouraging. It was stressful, but I was hanging on and keeping things positive.

The cars were still whizzing by and honking their horns at me, but I just smiled back. What was I to do? And actually, who was more foolish in the moment, them or me?

I knew it was a worn and leaky engine gasket that caused the car to stop. It often struggled in the kind of the stop-and-go traffic I was in. When Travis came, he had asked how long I had been there and I told him quite a while. He suggested starting the car again because maybe the car had cooled and would start. If it did, he would direct traffic to back me out. Then I could take the other interstate that would bring me around to the other side of Nashville (which had no delays) and get back home that way. As long as I didn't encounter any more stop-and-go traffic and I kept the car moving, I should be fine to get back home.

Now Travis can be a big intimidating guy to those who don't know him, and he walked straight out on the highway and made the traffic stop for me! The car did indeed start back up—he was right! I immediately backed out on the highway, and off I went!

There were so many blessings to this story. Our van could have broken down in the middle of the interstate going 75 mph with no shoulder to coast onto. Then we would have had to call a towing service and pay lots of money to get it back to our mechanic—but we didn't. All my friends didn't have to understand. They could have been mad, or I could have cried to them and had a meltdown, but they did understand and that made the challenges all the more endurable. Even though Steve's car died in stop-and-go traffic, it was a huge blessing to have Travis nearby to help me with his suggestions and directing of the traffic.

This wasn't a persecution (except for the name-calling from the drivers passing by), but this indeed was a *test*. One I was determined to pass, and I did! The enemy did not steal a thing from me that day. He received no victory in destroying my mood. I surrendered to the facts that were happening, but I didn't surrender my attitude. I had control over that and it all worked out.

> "Occasions make not a man fail, but show what the man is."
> ~Thomas Kempis

I was told later that my response was felt by Donna, Cindi, and Steve, and Travis and I laughed about it at church that coming week. They were all stressed for me, but it's in those situations that we can ignite the situation more based on how we respond to it.

I could have taken everyone's heads off because I was stressed out and hot! But I *chose* not to.

I had remembered what Paul was teaching us here. Instead I had friends praying for me, and I got through it and even laughed about it because it was so ridiculous, and there wasn't anything I could do about it anyway. Why not hand it over to God, because it all eventually works out in the end. It seems our circumstances don't matter as much as how we react to them.

If we do get down and discouraged, it's OK to ask God "Why?" And while it is OK to ask Him the hard questions, it's also OK for the answer to be simply "because."

- *Because* we live in a fallen world where evil and Satan reign at the present moment.
- *Because* the rain falls on the just and the unjust.
- *Because* the world system and its values are against Christ and all who follow Him.
- *Because* the world is groaning until the day of its redemption.
- *Because* Christ is not Lord in totality yet.[14]

In the meantime, we have to find our strength in Christ and know that difficulties, trials, attacks, and persecutions to our faith will come. But it's up to us as to how we'll choose to react.

Strengthening Our Hearts

It's important to note that Spiritual progress is always to be commended but it is never to be considered complete. Life is a continual journey. It would be good for us to remember that we are always "in-process" going through life.

Paul's prayer was that the believer's hearts would be strengthened. He realized that unless the heart is firmly established there will be no growth and development. It is the same with us. Faithful obedience to Christ will always result in misunderstandings and persecutions from those outside of the faith.

We will get it from all sides. It can be family members, friends, co-workers, classmates, etc. They say hurtful things because they don't get it. It comes from a place of ignorance. They might say, "You're waiting on the Lord? (in a mocking tone), just go get a new car and stop this nonsense of trying to get by!" You know what I mean. You fill in the blank with what has been said to you.

People give their "free" advice all of the time but only you know if you are following the Lord or not. It's important to be discerning by running everything you hear through prayer-time with the Lord and wait for His leading. As you hear His leading over you, you may still be met with opposition because people look only at what they see on the outside and not with a heart of faith.

Don't Compare Yourself

When we're walking a walk of faith and depending on God for provision we sometimes do the "comparison game" in our heads with others. Not everybody understands where God has called you to stand—not even your Christian friends. We hear the criticism that they speak over us and the doubt that gets sown in. And our faith gets shaky when the ones who are being critical of us seem to be the ones who look like they have it all together—especially on social media. We think since someone's life looks perfect their criticism of us must be right. That's simply not true! This is quite a deceiving tool. It takes the focus off of Christ who is the One who called you to this walk. Your focus is now on them—which left unchecked can turn into idol worship. You end up taking your eyes off of Christ and

> "Instruction does much, but encouragement is everything."
>
> ~Johann Wolfgang von Goethe

you find yourself miserable and confused, which was the goal of the enemy in the first place.

This is why encouragement is so important to us when our faith waivers. Encouragement becomes a source of strength in our relationships with one another. Encouragement gives us the ability to persevere. All of us are asked to walk a different walk in life and it can be difficult, so we need to be encouraging to each other and not a source of judgment. We have enough of that already.

I have four or five girlfriends I can call anytime there are days that are heavy on me and tell them I need them. They are right there with a good word and even some scripture. I am there for them as well. It's a two-way street. I consider myself a rich woman for having these relationships in my life. These types of relationships are needed if we are to survive.

It takes time and investment in each other to develop these types of relationships. If you are in need of one, start by getting plugged in at your local church. And if you are already part of a church, be proactive about getting involved there. Find those like-minded friends and work on those relationships because they yield real fruit and strength in your life.

"Therefore encourage one another and build each other up, just as in fact you are doing."
1 Thessalonians 5:11

Living in Purity

Paul calls the Christians to live holy lives; emphasizing sexual purity as we grow in our love for one another. He reminds them—and us—to live their own lives with care and confidence in Him. To live a life that pleases God.

This means when making these kinds of decisions ask yourself first; will this please God? We live in an overly sexualized world. Everything is about sex. The lines are blurred regarding morality these days with what we see played out before us in movies and television shows. If we see it enough, then we begin to adapt to that behavior. This is why we must make Him come first in all we do and in all we say.

If this is sounding prudish to you then that could be showing you that you have lowered your standards of what God wants for you. And if you've messed up in this area, then go to God and ask for forgiveness.

Forgiveness is there waiting for you and it's covered in His grace for you, too.

I'm not just talking about sex here either. What about our speech? How do you speak toward others? How do you act toward them? Are your jokes on the edge of vulgar? Can people really tell at work or even your neighbors tell if you live for God first and foremost? Do you act one way during the week and another way on Sunday? Only you can answer these questions. I have found it helps to live with this order in mind:

- God first,
- Family second,
- Job third.

This helps prioritize life when things get chaotic. God should always be first. Anytime I have confusion, I stop and think; where are my priorities? Is God first? Or if there is a decision with a job; is my family being considered? Sometimes we decide it's the job that is second. Even if it's ministry, these three points help clear up any confusion. God is first, family is second, and job is third. This just keeps things straight and it's easy to remember too.

Let me ask you; If Christ were to come visit you and He walked into your home, would you let Him scroll through the books and movies you keep in your home? Or are there a few you'd like to tuck away, so He won't see? Would you be comfortable watching your regular T.V. shows with Him sitting there next to you?

We have to live a life with this in mind. God comes first in all we do. In *all* we do! Let us be mindful of living a life that is pleasing to God. Let that be your goal.

> *"So that you may live a life worthy of the Lord and please Him in every way: bearing fruit in every good work, growing in the knowledge of God."*
> Colossians 1:10

CHAPTER 3

LIVING A LIFE OF READINESS

Reading assignment: 1 Thessalonians Chapters 4:13- 5:11

A Promised Return

Any of us who are parents or who have cared for a child will remember times when that child in our care was scared and insecure and didn't want us to leave. We would do our best to reassure the child with words of comfort like, "Don't worry, I'll be right back" or, "It won't be long, I'll be back soon."

I remember the first time I dropped off our son Kayce (our first born) for his very first Mothers Day Out program. I was excited for both of us until it was time to leave him. I was holding him and we were laughing and he seemed excited—until I started to hand him over to the child care worker. He pulled back and wrapped a death grip around my neck.

The worker said, "It will be OK," and I began to reassure him and promised him that I would come back. He just held on tighter. She looked at me calmly and smiled a reassuring smile at me and said, "This happens a lot." Then she reached for Kayce and pulled him off of me (more like peeled him off of me) and he began to scream so loud it was as if his arm had been severed off!

I just stood there in shock. Then the worker said to me, rather sternly, "Mrs. Grossman, you need to leave right now. He will be okay." Well, I did leave, but I wasn't okay. He was still screaming my name, "Mommy!

Mommy! Don't leave me! Mommy!" as I walked out. I could hear him all the way down the hall as I left the building. I sobbed and sobbed all of the way to the car and all the way driving home.

As soon as I came through the door I called them back (this was before cell phones) convinced he would still be hysterical and that this was a huge mistake. But he wasn't hysterical. He had settled down and made new friends and was playing with them. The next week went better and by the third week, Kayce was pushing me out the door saying, "Go Mommy!"

Dropping off Kayce was a test of my ability to surrender my heart and my child over to someone and trust that he would be okay. It was a risk that I needed to take to help Kayce trust that I would indeed come back for him. We both got through that first day and then there was such joy that came over him when I did come back just as I had promised!

Jesus spoke that way to us about His return. He said,

> *"Do not let your hearts be troubled. Trust in God; trust also in Me. …I will come back and take you to be with Me that you also may be where I am."*
> John 14:1-3

Christ promises to return to us! The return of Christ is the most mentioned event in all of Scripture. In fact, it is mentioned 300 times in the New Testament! [15] Christ's final words in Revelation are His promise of returning;

> *"Yes, I am coming soon!"*
> Revelation 22:20

He wanted to be sure we understood that. He wanted to inspire hope for us of His promise to return just like I had to promise Kayce that I would return.

Regarding Death

Even though the Thessalonians understood the Christian concept of death, that the believer is merely "asleep," death to the pagan culture was considered the complete and total end. There was nothing more that would await them. There was nothing to hope for: zip, zilch, nada—just utter hopelessness.

An evolutionist once shared his thoughts on a radio program about death: "We die, we rot." In a museum in St. Louis, Missouri, a picture of a farmer's wife was pictured standing next to a sod house with this quote: "Life's hard and then you die." A pagan tombstone from the time of Paul read, "I was not ... I became ... I am not ... I care not."

People who believe this way have no hope and no assurance, just despair.[16]

But we as Christians should not despair. Instead of sadness, we as believers in Christ are promised a resurrection and a reunion. We go from perishable to imperishable; from natural to spiritual; from dead to alive. A wonderful reunion awaits us!

When we face loss we don't grieve as the world does; we grieve with hope. We can know with assurance that the resurrection of our Christian loved ones is as sure as Christ's own resurrection after death.

"For we believe that Jesus died and rose again and so we believe that God will bring with Jesus those who have fallen asleep in Him."
1 Thessalonians 4:14

As Christians, in most cases we celebrate "a going home" event rather than a funeral.

This subject of death was considered a hot topic in Paul's day because let's remember, some of the actual witnesses to Christ's resurrection were still alive when this letter was written by Paul to the Thessalonians. It had only been a little over 20 years since Christ was crucified and raised from the dead so they could attest as eye witnesses to what they saw. This subject of death and how one should look at it was being discussed in many social circles.

Death to the Body

When we use the term "asleep," to Christians it means the death of the body and not the spirit. It's similar to what we learned when we studied James when he said,

> *"As the body without the spirit is dead."*
>
> James 2:26

A believer's soul goes immediately to be with the Lord when the body stops functioning. We may be sad when we lose a loved one but death should not bring fear to us. Let's look at what Paul said to the Corinthians about this:

> *"We are confident, I say, and would prefer to be away from the body and at home with the Lord."*
>
> 2 Corinthians 5:8

Again, there is a wonderful reunion that awaits us!

Who then is resurrected? The answer is *all* believers—the Church, Christ's bride. All believers living and dead will hear Christ's command as He comes.

> *"When He has brought out all His own, He goes on ahead of them, and His sheep follow Him because they know His voice."*
>
> John 10:4

Another promise is that we will be like Him:

> *"And just as we have borne the likeness of the earthly man, so shall we bear the likeness of the Man from heaven."*
>
> 1 Corinthians 15:49

> *"But we know that when Christ appears, we shall be like Him, for we shall see Him as He is."*
>
> 1 John 3:2

We are becoming Christ-like as we journey through this world. All of these testing times are transforming us as we learn to be more like Him, our Savior, our Lord, Jesus Christ.

The pain and loneliness experienced from the death of a loved one can be accompanied with great joy and hope by knowing that God indeed keeps His promises. We will see them again. But we must be willing to share in the hope we have about it too. It's too big to keep to ourselves. Getting the word out helps build Christ's church and enables those around us to avoid living in fear. Fear's goal is to cripple us.

When September 11, 2001 happened with the collapse of the Twin Towers in NYC, it brought back many to the church and renewed their hope and faith in Jesus. They were open to remembering the Gospel message. When moments like these occur, Christians have a great opportunity and *responsibility* to bring hope to others when death is present.

It is never "the end" when you believe in Jesus. That is a message that a hopeless world needs to hear and a reminder for your heart when times are full of grief. Even in the face of death, we all have witnessed people whose joy and hope far outweighs their grief and sadness. If you are faced with the death of a loved one right now, hold tight to this truth and be reminded of this hope. Remind yourself of God's great promises for resurrection and everlasting life.

Remember a wonderful reunion awaits us—*all* of us. He's coming back, Christ promises!

Understanding the Day of the Lord

When Christ does come back, Paul says we need to be awake and alert.

> *"Now, brothers and sisters, about times and dates we do not need to write to you, for you know very well that the Day of the Lord will come like a thief in the night."*
>
> 1 Thessalonians 5:2

What is the *Day of the Lord?*

It's the time when God will judge all the nations of the world, Israel will be purged, and Christ's kingdom will be ushered in. In Revelation chapters 6-19, John talks about all the end time events that must take place in order to usher in the New Jerusalem (If you want to know more of those chapters in a detailed account, I would encourage you to read my first book on the subject titled; *A Revelation of Love; A Comprehensive Study Companion to the Book of Revelation.* The details of these events are explained in full).

But at the time the Thessalonians received these letters from Paul, the apostle John had not yet been given the visions from the Lord that prompted him to write the book of Revelation. Jesus, however, did speak of Himself coming again and the Thessalonians began to worry because they were convinced the time was near.

Paul reminds the worried Thessalonians that they don't need times and dates because Christ's second coming will happen suddenly and it will happen without any warning. This is true for us today too. We will know the season, but not the specifics of the time.

Paul says to them,

> *"For you are fully aware that the Day of the Lord will come like a thief in the night. While people are saying, "Peace and security," destruction will come upon them suddenly, like labor pains on a pregnant woman, and they will not escape. But you, brothers, are not in the darkness so that this day should overtake you like a thief."*
>
> 1 Thessalonians 5:2-4

Remember, there's no need to be anxious because God is in control of all of this.

Walking In the Light

Every day we should remind ourselves that we are children of the light and Paul reminds us to walk in this light. We need to live everyday clothed in the spiritual armor of faith, love, and hope. In Biblical times a soldier's breastplate covered him from the neck to the waist, protecting his vital organs. Faith protects us inwardly, while love protects us outwardly. The hope of salvation is our helmet; it guards our minds and keeps us focused on Christ's return.

> **God expects us to be alert, awake, and to live in the light.**

Next, we need to live every day as if it's our last and live everyday for His glory! This is an attitude of expectation and readiness.

This is followed by living every day working diligently at whatever God gives us to do. While Christ may return tomorrow, we still plan for the years ahead, working at our assigned tasks and growing His kingdom. Don't slow down, keep running the race before you. And last, we need to live every day as a reflection of Christ. Be the light in a dark world. Remain balanced, cheerful, and stable, anticipating His return day-by-day. We may not know when, but Jesus *is* coming, so be His reflection of light and love.

> *"As water reflects the face, so one's life reflects the heart."*
>
> Proverbs 27:19

Faith, Hope, and Love

Faith, hope, and love are things that can be a part of our life. Our faith can lead us to trust God and know He is in charge. Our love gives us the motivation and energy to go the extra mile for another person. And our hope gives us comfort and encouragement when the world weighs us down.

It would help us to remember that a wonderful reunion awaits us! The Thessalonians and probably Paul himself expected Christ to return during their lifetime, but Paul never set dates. Jesus said no one but the Father can know the day or hour.

> *"But about that day or hour no one knows, not even the angels in heaven, nor the Son, but only the Father."*
>
> Mark 13:32

If anyone tries to tell you that they have the dates and times figured out, don't believe them because scripture is clear, *very* clear that no one knows. The Mayan Indians don't know, modern day prophets don't know, no one knows except the Father. We may know the season but never the actual date. So live ready and expectant, but live without anxiousness. Just trust in your loving Father that He has a complete plan ready to unfold at His appointed and perfect time.

Be Alert! Paul says we are not to be like others who are falling asleep:

> *"So then, let us not be like others, who are asleep, but let us be awake and sober."*
>
> 1 Thessalonians 5:6

Other translations say, be awake and serious. Falling asleep is a picture of what can happen to us spiritually, ethically, or morally if we are not watchful. Drowsiness begins and we become too comfortable. Soon our hearts become insensitive. One commentator said, "Spiritual drowsiness slowly paralyzes the spirit." The person who was once vibrant and wide awake in following Christ can become lethargic and lazy about issues of the spirit.

It happens all around us all the time. We need to be alert and sensitive to this so will it will not happen to us. It would be a crime against ourselves if we let this happen. So stay alert!

Perhaps you have been grappling with questions regarding Christ's return. Or perhaps you have dealt with, or are currently dealing with, the death of a loved one. Yes you must grieve, it's important that you allow yourself to. But remember there is hope within that grief and there is always hope for you, too. We hope with anticipation that God has prepared a place for us in heaven. There is such joy from that promised return! What a wonderful reunion awaits us to not only see our loved ones again but to see Jesus Christ, Son of God, our Savior, there too.

> "It is since Christians have largely ceased to think of the other world that they have become so ineffective in this one."
>
> ~C.S. Lewis

I firmly believe as we crossover from life to death that Christ is there with us and loving us. Yes He is judge, but only God knows the true heart of a person. Only He is omnipotent and can see when or why we hardened our hearts along the way or what happened back there in the past. Only He knows our secret places.

But He is not an angry God. He is a loving God who hears the cries of our hearts and only He can see in areas that we cannot. He is the ultimate Counselor and the ultimate Redeemer. If there is doubt in you regarding your loved one, seek God for that comfort and He will meet you there.

CHAPTER 4

JUSTICE, ENCOURAGEMENT AND WARNING

Reading assignment: Chapter's 1 Thess. 5:12 - 2 Thess. 1:12

> "The authority by which the Christian leader leads is not power but love, not force but example, not coercion but reasoned persuasion. Leaders have power, but power is safe only in the hands of those who humble themselves to serve."
>
> ~John Stott

Church Leadership

As Christians, we know that Christ brings changes in our lives and those changes can be challenging. Paul addresses some specific changes that need to be made. One of them is our behavior toward church leaders. Paul says,

> *"Now we ask you, brothers and sisters, to appreciate those who diligently work among you [recognize, acknowledge, and respect your leaders], who are in charge over you in the Lord and who give you instruction, [we ask that you appreciate them] and hold them in the highest esteem in love because of their work [on your behalf]. Live in peace with one another."*
>
> 1 Thessalonians 5:12-13 (AMP)

Honor is due to church leaders whether they are paid staff or lay people who give their time and energy to serve (i.e. elders, deacons, etc.). Spiritual leadership is difficult and weighted with responsibility. Because of that, these leaders are engaged in hard work. Paul encourages us to be supportive in every way

Living in Unity

Paul then turns our attention to the person sitting next to us (or across the aisle from us) and commands us to live in peace with one another. To live in peace means to go as far as possible to live in harmony with one another. I believe Paul is addressing the divisive spirit that can be present even in the healthiest of churches.

Wouldn't you agree that most people would not rob a bank or tell a blatant lie? They wouldn't ever sin against those clear commandments. Yet, the person who carries a divisive spirit into the church is acting in much the same way!

These are the people who find fault with everything from the leadership to the congregation. They don't seek to help fix a problem if there is one, they are just there to point out the weaknesses and speak as if they know it all. By speaking and acting this way, they end up bringing division among the people. They lie, by twisting scripture to make their point for their gain, and therefore steal from the people's spirits. It's rooted in selfish ambition which is rooted in pride and pride is rooted in unbelief.

You know the kind I'm talking about, right? People who act this way hurt not only themselves and others, but they also hurt the church as a whole.

Listen and Live In Peace

That's why we must listen to the teachings of Jesus and love our brothers and sisters in Christ. This is a *learned* skill. No one is perfect, and pastors are people too, but if we develop an attitude of a hardened heart toward our leaders and the church then we run the risk of becoming negative, cynical, and ultimately, unteachable.

Then the problem is more on you than on them. This can lead to you ending up being the one to leave the church, and isn't that the goal of the enemy: to divide and conquer? Instead, we are to strive to live in peace with one another.

> *"If it is possible, as far as it depends on you, live at peace with everyone."*
> Romans 12:18

"If it is possible ..." this scripture says.

Now I'm an optimistic person, but I'm a realist, too. Sometimes it's just not possible. Dale Carnegie said, "The best way to win an argument is to avoid it." This can be the right choice at times. Sometimes bad things happen to good people even in the church and sometimes we are forced to change churches to find that peace. And sometimes there is nothing wrong, we're just simply called by God to move on. But if there are challenges at your church, God will deal with that church if His Word is not being taught correctly or if the leadership is out of balance.

If you have to make this difficult choice, remember it is your role and responsibility to walk it out with as much peace as possible. God will not be mocked, so if there are real problems at your church for whatever reason, go to God with it. Trust Him with these matters and He will lead you through and show you what to do. Maybe you are to speak up or maybe you're to leave, but run it through the Lord as your trusted Advisor.

> "God will defend the truth spoken through the lips of liars"
> ~Randy Clark

God is about the heart so guard your heart against any hardness and division. If you're angry, then allow time to process your feelings, but don't stay there. Keep moving forward toward healing.

Paul goes on to give further instruction to the Thessalonians;

1. Don't be idle - This was a warning. There were those who were so certain of the imminent return of Christ that they became lazy in their daily living. We can do the same. We can become too idle ourselves and become too absorbed in the daily routine and forget that there is God's work to do. We can get so comfortable that we fail to use our gifts, our time, and our lives for others.

An Alaskan dog musher described the differences between the huskies in the straps of the sled. He said that some of them are known as "dishonest" dogs. They learn how to fake it because they pretend they are working hard by leaning against the harness without really pulling.[17]

Maybe we should examine ourselves to see if we are "dishonest" by failing to do our share in doing Christ's work.

2. The timid are to be encouraged - These were the people who had become discouraged, maybe even depressed, because of the difficult circumstances they were facing. They began feeling that they couldn't walk the walk of faith anymore.

These types of people need our help. They don't need warnings but encouragement. Are we encouraging to others? I know when my circumstances get too heavy to bear a word of encouragement means a lot to me. Sometimes it's all I need.

3. The weak are to be helped - Paul is talking about the spiritually weak. This applies to us today. The church is filled with people who may struggle with ongoing sins that continually defeat them. Because of it all, they may lack the courage to find it difficult to trust God. Our encouragement may be just the thing to give them a renewed hope and that will help them break the cycle they're in.

4. Have patience - Everyone should be dealt with in patience and with love. This is the cornerstone that will help us to be patient ourselves.

> *"Love is patient…"*
>
> 1 Corinthians 13:4

When I'm struggling with insecurities, I want people to be patient with me, so I *need* to be patient with others. I also love that this is a gift from the Lord to us. We don't earn it; it is given lovingly and freely. So handle it respectfully.

Our Inner Attitudes

Next, Paul addresses our inner attitudes. We should be mindful to;

> *"Be joyful always; pray continually, give thanks in all circumstances, for this is God's will for you in Christ Jesus."*
>
> 1 Thessalonians 5:16-18

"Be joyful always" is short and to the point. The key however, is the word *always*. Paul meant this literally. The Christian's joy is not bound by circumstances or hindered by difficulties. Paul found joy even while in jail! But it is a choice.

Having joy is a deliberate response that allows us to focus on the grace and goodness of God. That's where we find true joy. We find it in Him and not in our circumstances. Sometimes we can't change our circumstances at all. For example, we can't change the family we were born into. But, we can change ourselves within those circumstances, and then we can find the joy that lies there that only comes with having a relationship with God Almighty Himself.

When Paul said to, *"pray continually,"* I believe he was referring to our attitude of prayer and our reverence to God. Sometimes we are to pray on our knees for periods of time for a specific reason. For example, Daniel felt he was to pray many times a day.

> *"Now when Daniel knew that the document was signed, he entered his house (now in his roof chamber he had windows open toward Jerusalem); and he continued kneeling on his knees three times a day, praying and giving thanks before his God, as he had been doing previously."*
>
> Daniel 6:10

We know this was for a specific reason but our approach in prayer should also include respect for our relationships and our responsibilities. Prayer should always maintain a constant attitude of being in God's presence. It's a countenance we carry with us.

> *"Pray in the Spirit at all times, with every kind of prayer and petition. To this end, stay alert with all perseverance in your prayers for all the saints."*
>
> Ephesians 6:18

You can pray while folding clothes, or driving to work or showering, etc. My point is to carry the attitude and countenance of prayer with you at all times.

Giving *"thanks in all circumstances"* requires trust in the sovereignty of Christ. We have to first believe that God is present in all of those circumstances whether they are easy or hard, joyful or sorrowful.

We are to do God's will and God's will is that we are to be joyful, prayerful, and thankful in all of our circumstances. There is a lesson that can be learned from the trials we go through. We just need to ask God to show it to us. Going through the process shapes us into the likeness of Christ and isn't that the ultimate goal anyway? That is why when Paul sat in jail, through his thankfulness, he could find the joy he needed which transcended his circumstances because his focus was to be more like Christ. That's all he cared about.

All of these points build on each other. The Christians joy is not dependent on circumstances. It comes from what Christ has done for us. John reminds us what Jesus said after speaking about keeping His commandments:

> *"I have told you this so that My joy may be in you and that your joy may be complete."*
>
> John 15:11

Keeping Our Spiritual Integrity

As we are learning and growing in our inner attitudes Paul reminds us to be mindful of keeping our spiritual integrity. Remember, the Thessalonians were asking about the Day of the Lord and there was anxiety over it.

The attitudes Paul that shares are the same for us today because there is a growing darkness in our present-day world. There is a defiant spirit coupled with humanistic attitudes and people are following all sorts of things because of their ignorance to God's Word. We must be careful! We are children of the day and not children of the night.

Paul mentions not to put out the Spirit's fire either. This means do not douse the Spirit's influence in our lives. That only begins to happen when we let doubt in.

> **The joy and peace we desire lies within us to unlock, so be mindful of your inner attitude always.**

The Holy Spirit Himself cannot be put out because He is God. However, we can stifle His work in our life if we're not careful. We have the power to squelch and grieve the Spirit when we do not reach for the attitudes and graces which are His.

I'm speaking about the Gifts of the Spirit which are listed in 1 Corinthians 12. Let's get more context here:

> *"Brothers and sisters, I want you to know about the gifts of the Holy Spirit. You know that at one time you were unbelievers. You were somehow drawn away to worship statues of gods that couldn't even speak. So I want you to know that no one who is speaking with the help of God's Spirit says, "May Jesus be cursed." And without the help of the Holy Spirit no one can say, "Jesus is Lord." There are different kinds of gifts. But they are all given to believers by the same Spirit. There are different ways to serve. But they all come from the same Lord.*
>
> *There are different ways the Spirit works. But the same God is working in all these ways and in all people.*
>
> *The Holy Spirit is given to each of us in a special way. That is for the good of all. To some people the Spirit gives a message of wisdom. To others the same Spirit gives a message of knowledge. To others the same Spirit gives faith. To others that one Spirit gives gifts of healing.*
>
> *To others he gives the power to do miracles. To others he gives the ability to prophesy. To others he gives the ability to tell the spirits apart. To others he gives the ability to speak in different kinds of languages they had not known before. And to still others he gives the ability to explain what was said in those languages.*
>
> *All the gifts are produced by one and the same Spirit. He gives gifts to each person, just as he decides."*
>
> 1 Corinthians 12:1-11

The Spirit's fire is quenched when His presence is ignored and His guidance and conviction doesn't reach our hearts. The Holy Spirit ends up being suppressed and ultimately rejected.

> *"Do not extinguish the Spirit. Do not treat prophecies with contempt."*
> 2 Thessalonians 5:19-20

Paul also says we are not to treat prophecies with contempt. Some translations say not to "despise" them. The Greek meaning for this is, "to act as if the thing in question means nothing." Everything we do in the world has a spiritual component to it.

Please don't treat these gifts of the Holy Spirit with contempt or despise them because they are gifts to us.

Finding Balance with God's Gifts

In the church of Thessalonica some of the believers were so worried about the misuse of the charismatic gifts that they allowed none of them (While just the opposite was happening in Corinth). Sounds like many churches we know of today. We have to be careful with this!

The ignorance that people have in regards to the knowledge of God's Word will leave them vulnerable to be enticed by dark spirits acting as spirits of light. We need to be in tune with the Holy Spirit's leading in our life to filter whether what is being said is coming from God or not. The only way to do that is to have a personal relationship with Jesus Christ.

As we invite Christ into our lives we usher in the Holy Spirit to live inside of us to guide and counsel us along the way. He will let us know if we're being deceived or not. But that can't happen without having a relationship with Him first and learn to hear His voice.

Regarding Prophecies

Scholars are divided today on whether prophecies—which are a direct revelation from God—are still God's gift to the church or whether these ceased with the completion of the New Testament. I'm not telling you what to believe, but I am telling you to seek the Lord on this if you are unresolved on this issue.

Many of us have or know someone who has gone to see a psychic of some kind and had their fortune read or the tarot cards read to them. I know someone who went to a psychic and the psychic brought up a memory of my friend's childhood and the name of her next door neighbor! My friend was blown away and for years gravitated toward mysticism because it excited her. However, through the years it pulled her away from the things of God, which is what happens when we seek other spiritual things outside of Him.

We need to be careful and discerning here. Spirits may have knowledge but some of those spirits are dark spirits! That's why they deceive people. I'm not at all surprised that this spirit knew things about my friend. But she didn't have the discernment of the things of God and allowed herself to be tempted and intoxicated by the wonders of the darkness. Soon church and Christianity itself were not exciting enough and she only sought things of a mystic nature. She lost herself along the way and now lives a life without the true power of God. He's just the God of Sunday mornings now, who lives at Fifth and Main.

> Studying prophecy is good, but it is better to live in obedience to the prophetic Word of God.

Test Everything

Finally, Paul says to test everything. The word "everything" is universal. It leaves nothing free from examination by spiritual standards. This clear purpose of testing is to hold on to the good and avoid every kind of evil and you do that through discernment and prayer.

Our son was on a mission trip recently and traveled along with an organization of people he didn't know. One night, out of the blue, they began to speak a word of knowledge over everyone. One of them focused directly on our son. He felt singled out and disturbed by this because he didn't know this guy's background and was trying to process what was being said about him and whether to believe it or not.

He came to us when he got back and shared what had happened. Since he has a close walk with his heavenly Father, we told him to put it to prayer and the Holy Spirit would show him what was of God and what was not. He did just that and that helped him find clarity and peace.

Here's my point: run everything you hear through the Holy Spirit for confirmation. Sometimes the best, well-meaning intentions are not from God but from man or worse, from a place of darkness. If you're in line with seeking the Holy Spirit's guidance though, you'll know whether to keep it as truth for you or not. The Holy Spirit will never deceive you so test all of what is being said so you won't be deceived. Paul wants us to live with these points and make them habits in our lives, because the more we seek the Holy Spirit for guidance the more we'll recognize His leading in us.

When we apply all of these spiritual attitudes to our lives this enables us to live a life so that God can count us worthy of His kingdom. I want that, don't you?

Paul's Warnings in His Second Letter

Paul then wrote a second letter to the Thessalonian church not long after the first letter was written. The messengers who delivered the first letter had returned with the news that the church was hearing unbalanced and distorted teachings about Christ's second coming. So Paul addresses this in this second letter and continues to encourage them in the face of persecution. It seemed that the persecutions had been intensifying.

> "Out of our beliefs are born deeds; out of our deeds we form habits; out of our habits grows our character; and on our character we build our destiny."
> ~Henry Hancock

Even so, Paul saw that the unbalanced and distorted teachings were a far greater threat! They could have undermined their grasp of God's foundational message of truth and that *was* dangerous.

Paul points out that their faith, love, and endurance was under intense persecution:

> *"...and a result you will be counted worthy of the kingdom of God, for which you are suffering."*
>
> 2 Thessalonians 1:5

When we show strength in the face of adversity through our faith it shows the world that God is victorious. And this is a foreshadowing of Christ's final conquest at the Second Coming. It points others to the bigger picture going on around us.

God Does Care

When we endure hardships, trials, and even heartaches—especially the ones undeserved—we are sometimes tempted to think that God doesn't care. I know all of us have been guilty of this from time to time. But it is a lie. It doesn't match up with the character of God and who He is.

The Thessalonians felt that God didn't care either. They wondered how God could permit such trouble when the believers were only doing what was right. We've all felt that way at times but we need to remember and trust that God operates from a different perspective. We don't know what all is going on around us in the spirit realm. Jesus warned us and made this clear when He said in John 16:

"In this world you will have trouble..."

If we truly believe scripture and what it says then we have to see that God is a good, good Father and He is all about loving us. He wants good things for us! Would any of us be able to surrender our own son to be beaten and given up as a sacrifice for an unbelieving world simply because of love? When we stop and really think about that point, believing that God is uncaring and unconcerned just doesn't line up anymore.

We can trust, truly trust, in His character by holding on to the complete verse:

"...but take heart I have overcome the world!"

John 16:33

Unfair Treatment

When there is unfair treatment and hostile circumstances, God can strengthen His children from within so that their faith grows even stronger.

Let's remember, Paul was not on a vacation while he was away writing these letters to the Thessalonians. He was being chased and persecuted. He had a maturity in his faith so that he had stopped asking God *why* all the time. He trusted God and therefore was able to encourage others to stay strong.

Do you trust God enough with your circumstances? Do you trust in His sovereignty over your life? Do you trust that He is a good Father for you?

Paul was able to help the Thessalonians with the truth regarding Christ's return and remind them of God's true character.

Throughout the Bible, from the Garden of Eden to the Day of the Lord, it reveals God acting in accordance with His essential characteristic of love.

Think about it: we never see God hate, slander, or steal. He is never rude or abusive to any living thing. It is man that is cruel to man. Four fifths (4/5) of all human suffering is caused by the behavior of man to man. That's a lot of suffering that we are causing each other but blaming God for.

> "Rather than being horrified by human neglect or hatefulness, we want to blame God for the things that undoubtedly grieve Him, too."
>
> ~C.S. Lewis

Let's remember that when God speaks, it is as Creator, Loving Savior, and Merciful Judge. We may not understand all His ways but that's more about us. His love for us is and should be beyond our questioning.

Paul Gives Another Warning

> *"He will punish those who do not know God and do not obey the gospel of our Lord Jesus. They will be punished with everlasting destruction and shut out from the presence of the Lord and from the glory of His might."*
>
> 2 Thessalonians 1:8-9

This is a serious point Paul is making and a lot of people get hung up on this one. They ask how can a "merciful judge" punish those who do not know God? Weren't we just talking about Him being a *good* God?

First off, this scripture is referring to those who know God but refuse to recognize Him. The Gospel invites us into the acceptance. The rejection of it is disobedience.

This is a royal invitation and it is a choice. It is always a choice to respond to the promise of eternal life through Christ or reject the good news of salvation. But just to be clear; the consequences of a "no" choice are everlasting destruction and a separation from a God who is love and that is *forever*—and forever is a long time! Are you willing to risk that?

C. S. Lewis pondered this point and wrote a book entitled "The Great Divorce." In the book, he tells the story of a number of people in hell who take a bus trip to heaven to see if they would rather be there. One by one, many of the characters realize they do not want heaven, so they return to hell. You see, they prefer hell, as Satan did in John Milton's "Paradise Lost."

The attitude for all was that it was better to reign in hell rather than to serve in heaven.

Remember, Satan personifies hostility against God. He's powerful and he's thoroughly evil. Everything about Satan's kingdom has to do with death and destruction, darkness and sadness. He is the "father of lies" Jesus says.

But, let's be clear, he is *not* God's *equal* counterpart either. I want to remind you again, that Satan is a created being. God could snap his fingers and he could be gone. But God has a plan for this world and the coming of a new one. On that day, he (Satan) and those who stand with him will be destroyed.

Second, I believe God takes no pleasure and feels no inward joy over having to punish this way. No one, including God Himself, rejoices over it. But God is a just God bound to His own laws, rules and covenants. The punishment of true wickedness is righteous, holy, fair, and necessary. And Just. The coming of the Lord means condemnation yes, but it also means His glorification among all of His people too! God has begun good purposes in you and He will bring them to completion through every act prompted by faith.

This was good for the Thessalonians to hear and is a good reminder for us, too.

Keep the Faith

Let's remember that the church belongs to Christ. We should never consider the church "ours" in a possessive or controlling sense. Decisions we make in regard to our local congregation should be motivated by our desire to glorify the Lord through our gatherings. We should all be heavenly minded and live with a kingdom living attitude.

True spirituality is never in a holding position. We either progress or we lose ground. We should not be surprised by difficulties when they come because scripture is clear that we will have them. We are only here on earth for a short time and then comes eternity. With that in mind, we should order our lives with the understanding that God will judge all people some day.

And by the way, there *is* a heaven and there *is* a hell. Don't let anyone fool you. This knowledge should motivate us to share the Gospel with others and begin praying for their salvation.

This commentary excerpt clearly and concisely sums things up:

> "We must come to understand that the "good" which God is determined to accomplish in our lives is to make us like Christ. We can live above our circumstances. Every wonderful or crummy thing that happens to us is not excluded from the creative finger of God. Nothing in our experience is wasted. He is committed to our transformations and will use everything at His disposal to shape our character, faith, obedience, and love.
>
> When we embrace this kind of good, we are released from the small ambitions of this life. The worthiness of our life does not depend on the success of our efforts but on becoming more and more like Jesus Christ. God is in charge of the creative process by which we are being changed into the likeness of His Son. Our part is to surrender in faith, believing the declarations of God to be true and the character of God to be indisputably good."[18]

Helen Lemmel's words simplify all of this in her beautiful hymn, *Turn Your Eyes Upon Jesus*:

> "Turn your eyes upon Jesus
> Look full in His wonderful face.
> And the things of the world
> Will grow strangely dim,
> In the light of His glory and grace."[19]

CHAPTER 5

STANDING IN TRUTH

Reading assignment: 2 Thessalonians Chapters 2-3

> "If we refuse to practice, it is not God's grace that fails when a crisis comes, but our own nature…God regenerates us and puts us in contact with all His divine resources but He cannot make us walk according to His will."
>
> ~Oswald Chambers

Warnings about hurricanes, a mounting disease, or social turmoil make us all alert to those potential dangers. And our concerns are valid because these types of dangers have proven to be deadly and devastating.

It's the same with a false rumor. Remember the fable; "The Boy Who Cried "Wolf!"? This boy had lied and fooled the town so much by crying out "Wolf!" that when a wolf really was there no one believed him.

This is what Paul was concerned about. These false teachings that were going around were frightening the Thessalonians. The false rumor being spread was that Christians had missed the return of Christ. They were upset about this and Paul's letter helped to correct this misconception and add insight for them which brought hope.

We have the advantage of time today. Over 2,000 years of time and history give us a greater understanding of prophetic teachings that we can gain understanding from.

The Thessalonians didn't have that luxury.

We as Christians need to maintain a balance between knowing, doing, waiting, working, and living responsibly as we expectantly await the Lord's return just like the Thessalonians did. Godly living requires balance and that requires self-discipline and purposeful choices. We do not advance in our Christian faith automatically; it takes determination and making right choices along the way.

False Teachings and Fake Reports

At the core of the false teachings circulating was that the Day of the Lord had already arrived. This may have been spoken as a false prophecy, a fake report, or a forged letter written by Paul's Jewish enemies.

> "The great value of the doctrine of the Second Coming is that it guarantees that history is going somewhere."
>
> ~William Barclay

They were saying the end was near, Christ had already come, and the plans for the future were needless. This may explain why Paul addressed the idleness that some of the Thessalonians were experiencing.

Paul explains to them that before the Lord's return there will be a rebellion and the "man of lawlessness" will be revealed. This will be Satan's final effort to overthrow God's purposes. Yet it is God, and only God, that has set the time:

> *"But about that day or hour no one knows, not even the angels in heaven, nor the Son, but only the Father."*
>
> Mark 13:32

Paul explains that this man of lawlessness will come and will attempt to do two things:

1. He will exalt himself and oppose everything that is worshiped, setting himself up as God in the temple.
2. He will try to utterly confuse the understanding of truth.

The point Paul is making is that this man has not yet come, so therefore the second coming of Christ cannot have taken place!

The Man of Lawlessness

This man is the antichrist, whom the prophet Daniel refers to as the *"little horn"* (Daniel 7:8), and John calls him *"the beast"* (Revelation 13:12). The antichrist is someone who deceives others and denies that Jesus is the Christ. That's why he is the *anti*-Christ.

Throughout church history, many have attempted to identify this "man of lawlessness." Many thought that the Roman emperor Gaius Julius Caesar (emperor from AD 37 to AD 41) might have been this lawless man because he wanted to be worshiped by setting up a statue of himself in the temple of Jerusalem.[20] His unexpected death by assassination halted the temple desecration. One can surely see how this may have influenced the Thessalonian Christians to believe this was the man of lawlessness and that the end was near.

Near the end of Paul's life, some thought it was the Emperor Nero. Nero claimed that he was god incarnate and promoted worship of himself. His extreme cruelty to Christians led people to believe that they were indeed in the last days.

After his death, and the deaths of the apostles, many early church leaders believed Nero himself would be resurrected from the dead and continue his terrible rule culminating in declaring himself god.[21]

The point is many people will be deceived in the last days. Radio and TV programs often discuss the "signs and wonders." Wonders don't prove Christ's presence. Believing the truth of the Scriptures does. If we seek the gifts more than the Giver then we're guilty of idol worship.[22]

> **When we don't have all the facts, distorted information can be dangerous.**

The only way we can discern the difference is through studying and learning God's Word. This is the truth and the foundation from which we can, and should, stand.

Knowledge of God's Word

It is also important that when you listen to any kind of teacher or preacher you run it through the Word of God whether there is a question or not. Check the context from which they are pulling their points from. Write down the scripture references given and look them up and see for yourself what it says. The Holy Spirit will tell you if something doesn't match up.

You see, any scripture can be taken out of context to make almost any right or wrong point. This is exactly what Satan did with Jesus in the desert. Satan knows scripture *very* well and he will take it and twist it to manipulate and confuse you. That is why we need to understand the "why's" and "when's" of scripture. It helps to know the foundation from which the teachers and preachers are speaking from.

Listen to the Holy Spirit's prompting in you because deception may occur—just like Paul experienced. He was preaching the truth but his enemies were distorting it. It's still happening today. The truth may be being preached but deceivers are tearing down the truth.

What do you really believe? We need to know the truth in our hearts as well as our heads. In-depth Bible studies are vitally important. Don't just let yourself be spoon fed by someone else's opinion of what they think the Word says. Make sure they are backing it up with scripture and let the Holy Spirit be your ultimate teacher. Read the passages for yourself. Look up the Hebrew or Greek meanings of key words. It will deepen your knowledge and also your love for God.

Through the centuries believers in various lands have suffered prolonged periods of persecutions and deprivations and believed that the day of the Lord was upon them. But any teaching about the timing of the day of the Lord and the identity of the "man of lawlessness" must be carefully examined. To avoid being deceived, we must

> *"...hold firm to the trustworthy Word as taught."*
>
> Titus 1:9

John says that what he included in his Gospel is sufficient for us to find salvation in Christ:

> *"Jesus did many other signs in the presence of the disciples, which are not written in this book; but these are written so that you may believe that Jesus is the Christ, the Son of God, and that by believing you may have life in His name."*
>
> John 20:30-31 (ESV)

We are also assured that

> *"[God's] divine power has given us everything we need for life and godliness through our knowledge of Him."*
>
> 2 Peter 1:3

Because Jesus' teachings are constantly being distorted and mixed with falsehoods we must base our understanding of the last days on what we find in Scripture. Our trustworthy God has made sure that the knowledge contained in the Bible is sufficient for all the challenges we face.

The Humanistic Spirit

Today, right now, there dwells a "spirit of the antichrist" here in the world. Humanistic teachings are all around us. In fact, the "humanistic spirit" itself says, *Man is god*.

Think of the lure of Eastern religions and New Age thinking. These have the belief that we can work our way to perfection and set ourselves up as our own god. Or there's the belief that if we will just do more good than bad, we will make it to heaven.

Yet we know these statements are false.[23]

> *"For all have sinned and fall short of the glory of God."*
>
> Romans 3:23

> *"For the wages of sin is death, but the gift of God is eternal life in Christ Jesus our Lord."*
>
> Romans 6:23

The New Age, humanistic thinking is all about "me first." There is no one pointing people toward Jesus, just themselves. This attitude or spirit is nothing new. Isaiah warned us all about it:

> *"These people come near to Me with their mouth*
> *and honor Me with their lips,*

but their hearts are far from Me.
Their worship of Me is based on merely human rules they have been taught.
Therefore once more I will astound these people
with wonder upon wonder;
the wisdom of the wise will perish, the intelligence of the intelligent will vanish."
Woe to those who go to great depths
to hide their plans from the Lord,
who do their work in darkness and think,
"Who sees us? Who will know?"

Isaiah 29:13-15

Today people are identifying themselves through the labels that they give themselves. "I'm gay," "I'm transgender," "I'm bi-sexual" for example. Let me just say you are *not a label*. No one is a label. Your identity lies with Christ Jesus. Even with the struggle of addiction, the core of the fight inside is not the drugs, alcohol, porn (you fill in the blank), but the identity of who you are in Christ!

All of the political correctness that is prevalent today has kept the truth from being spoken. This has been blown out of proportion with our labels instead of a focus on our identity in Christ. A label is just that: a label. There is no such thing as a "loser," just someone who's lost. There is no such thing as a "jerk" etc… We are not our mistakes, our desires, or our appetites.

Our true identity goes so much deeper but you can't know who you are until you know *Whose* you are. You are a son and daughter of the most-high God and an heir to the throne! That is who you are AND Whose you are!

What is actually happening is that we are *resisting* the fear of God and *embracing* the fear of man instead. The result is rebellion. It is a rebelliousness that shows up to any kind of authority and that gives way to a spirit of entitlement.

I have seen so many rebellious comments toward authority, whether it's our government or our boss, the comments are there. Just think about the degrading posts or nasty comments on social media during the recent elections in

> **You can't know "who" you are until you know "Whose" you are.**

the United States. And then we wonder why we have a culture of youth who don't respect authority—they've learned it from us!

This spirit is a self focused spirit that says it's all about "me." When the enemy speaks he makes it all about inward things like "I," "me," "my" that is used over and over in our thought and speech. Jesus however, is all about the *outward* things like,

> *"Love your neighbor"*
>
> Mark 12:31

> *"Serve one another"*
>
> Galatians 5:13

> *"Encourage one another"*
>
> 1 Thessalonians 5:11

> *"Give thanks in all circumstances"*
>
> 1 Thessalonians 5:18

We need to pause and listen to ourselves. But there is hope from this self-centered evil:

> *"God cannot be tempted by evil and He Himself tempts no one."*
>
> James 1:13

Let's go back to the character of God.

Knowing God's Character

God does not lie to unbelievers but the "father of lies" does. Everything Satan speaks is a lie. The Holy Spirit does not prompt people into faith of the "man of lawlessness." God simply releases them to the full consequences of their choices.

Paul tells us in 2 Thess. 2:11 that because of their deliberate rejection of the truth God allows sin to punish sinful behavior.

We also know:

> *"Whoever believes in Him is not condemned, but whoever does not believe stands condemned already because they have not believed in the name of God's one and only Son. This is the verdict: Light has come into the world, but people loved darkness instead of light because their deeds were evil."*
>
> John 3:18-19

The truth is being watered down. Christianity is being homogenized by some church leaders who are more afraid of preaching the black and white of God's truth for fear losing members in the congregation. Now that's resisting the fear of God and embracing the fear of man.

There was a woman who was "uninvited" to speak at a church because the Biblical Truth she spoke about was too uncomfortable for them to hear. She wrote a loving blog post sharing her concern about this fear of man over fearing God.[24] Another example is we hear of truth being preached with a spirit of condemnation! This is equally bad and very harmful. No wonder we have issues with people who hate church because it can be damaging and distorted.

We need to have a keen eye and a sharp ear for the Fruits of the Spirit in a teacher or preacher (referencing Galatians 5). These need to be present in delivering God's Word. The heart of God's Word, which is truth and love, should show through. Remember, there is no condemnation in Christ Jesus! If there is conviction on people, then the Holy Spirit is bringing that on. You just continue to be Christ-like, obedient and be full of loving kindness as you share His truth to all who will listen and leave the rest to the Holy Spirit.

> "God cannot be tempted by evil and He Himself tempts no one."

When is Enough, Enough?

Suppose someone offered you limitless and restraint free fun for ten minutes. You would be free to indulge yourself with no limits, rules and laws, and you could even ignore the feelings of others!

I presume you would consider such an offer to be foolish. After all, there is more to life than just ten minutes, right?

What if the offer was extended to an hour of doing whatever you feel like doing, whatever passions, or whatever desires compel you? Take what you want, use whatever you see, cater to your every whim. It's still foolish for even an hour, right?

What about for a day, or a month, or even a year?

I think you'd still argue; "Life is more than a day, a month or a year."

So what about 20 years? The true question is: If it is wrong to give into selfish, inconsiderate behaviors and sin for ten minutes, where does such conduct become reasonable? Or said another way: at what point is self-indulgence worth it? The answer is never. In the light of eternity, sin is never worth any of our time.[25]

We must be heavenly minded and not earthly bound in all we do. Paul wrote to the Thessalonians encouraging and commending them for their endurance in suffering and persecution. They were thinking heavenly minded thoughts rather than crumbling under the pressures of a godless society or giving into their cultures standards.

> **In the light of eternity, sin is never worth any of our time.**

They chose to say "no" to the world and to say "yes" to righteousness. They understood that life consisted of more than a day, a month, a year etc… They responded in faith to God's grace by committing themselves to Christ's commands and holiness because they understood there would be glory and reward for doing so. They understood that for those who indulged in a self-consumed life, giving no mercy, there would be judgment.[26]

The lesson is still the same today.

Standing Firm in Truth

Paul ends his letter with guidance on how to stand firm in the truth. He says to:

- Believe the Word *"…belief in the truth"* (2 Thess. 2:13)
- Hold to the Word *"…hold to the teachings we passed on to you whether by word of mouth or by letter."* (2 Thess. 2:15)
- Share the Word *"…that the message of the Lord may spread rapidly and be honored, just as it was with you."* (2 Thess. 3:1)

God loves us so much He set us apart for Himself and sent His Son to die for us! Jesus was the Son of God who modeled the love and character of God. We need to believe, trust, and open ourselves to Him. He can handle the frustrations, doubts, and discouragements that get us down. We're not meant to shoulder them all alone.

Jesus said:

> *"Take My yoke upon you and learn from Me; for I am gentle and humble in heart, and you will find rest for your souls. For My yoke is easy and My burden is light."*
>
> Matthew 11:29-30

Surrender it to Him and lay it at the altar. Obey His word in attitude and in action.

Read God's Word Daily

Read God's Word daily and let it sink deep into your heart. Work at following His teachings consistently. Paul encourages the Thessalonians to;

> *"...never tire of doing what is right."*
>
> 2 Thessalonians 3:13

The fight to stand for what s right is getting more intense with each passing day so live with this in mind to please God and not man.

Be Supportive

If you continue to feel that heavy load on your shoulders get around encouragers to help you stay strong and that can keep you standing through the trials in your life. In turn, *you* can be the encourager for others because you don't know what they might be carrying. Your words carry power so use them for lifting others up.

Like I said at the beginning of this book, life is like a barrel of monkeys: We are lifting someone up as we are being lifted up and together we will help each other through all of our trials that come our way.

As Paul ends his letter to the Thessalonians, he not only gives them guidance on how to stand firm in truth, but to live out that truth and avoid idleness.

Even if we are being tested we must stand firm in believing the Word of God and holding fast to its truths. We must test our motives and actions against it. We must hold to our standards of our brothers, sisters, and especially ourselves to a higher standard that will ultimately glorify our Lord.

What will Jesus say when He comes for you? Will you be ready? Will He be pleased? What will your attitudes and actions on that day reveal about your readiness? Only you can answer that, but my hope is that no matter what you are going through, you will stand firm in the truth before you.

The Most Important Decision to Make

If you have never accepted Jesus as your Savior, or if you're not even sure you have, I hope you will do so right now. We all may be experiencing challenges and trials of many kinds, but there is a bigger one coming at you that is between good and evil without this choice. This is the fight for your heart and mind. *That* is the true battlefield! This is about choosing to live in eternity with Christ, or not.

> "The devil wrestles with God, and the field of battle is the human heart."
>
> ~Fyodor Dostoyevsky

If you haven't accepted Jesus Christ as your Lord and Savior then I pray you do so now. This decision is the *most important* decision you'll ever make—*ever!*

If you haven't or aren't sure will you pray and repeat these words with me?

Dear Jesus,
I accept You now into my heart as my Savior and Lord. I believe that You are Lord! I believe that God sent Jesus His Son, to come and die for me on the cross so that my sins could be forgiven. There is no other God but You, and there is no other way to heaven except through Your Son, Jesus Christ. Forgive me of my sins Lord. Wash me clean with Your love and come to live in my heart forever.
Amen

Welcome to the family of God! You are not alone and you are not to carry your burdens alone either. Surrender them to Him because He can handle them.

Now, I want to encourage you to go and find a church and become a part of a community of God which will help you continue to grow in the Father. When you're ready, consider being baptized as an outward expression of your faith.

Congratulations! I can hear heaven rejoicing even now.

> *"In the same way, I tell you, there is rejoicing in the presence of the angels of God over one sinner who repents."*
>
> Luke15:10

We find our strength and our hope to endure anything we go through with understanding His Word, finding our identity through it, and ultimately our purpose.

Trust and surrender to the One who will carry you through this and fine tune you along the way.

EPILOGUE

Remember when I told you about my parents dying of two different terminal diseases at the same time when you first began reading?

There's a little more to the story I want to share with you now.

My mother died a year and three months before my dad did. So there was no time to grieve for her. We all had to pick ourselves up by our boot straps and keep going with crisis #2: my dad.

Six weeks before he died, my dad ended up marrying his caretaker. He was 69, she was 41. It was a classic case of someone taking advantage of an invalid. There was pressure and stress from this unnatural union and yes, she was very dysfunctional.

On the evening of my dad's death, she came back to the house and there was a fight between my siblings and her. It was electrifying and stressful with lots of drama! I had to leave to get Kayce, our son (who was now 4 years old) from where he was staying with a friend of mine. I was so frustrated and upset from the fight that had just happened, I cried and screamed and banged on the steering wheel as I drove. Everything came to the surface.

Finally, I pulled off of the road onto a dirt road which faced some woods which were about 50 yards away and parked for a moment. It was dusk and I was done emotionally. I was having a talk with God and saying I was through. Life shouldn't be this hard and I was beginning to partner with the lie that He didn't really exist. Who is this God who just wants praise but gives no mercy or grace? My heart began to harden. I wouldn't let myself be vulnerable again. I would pull inward and take care of myself - alone. As I gazed out my window with my eyes swollen from crying, I decided that when I got back to Tennessee I would give away all of my bibles. I was done with church, Christianity, and God. This was just too much pain.

Then all of a sudden there was a knock at my driver's side window. I thought to myself before I turned my head that, "Great, now I'm going to die on an isolated dirt road." As I turned my head I saw a woman with a kind smile who had gotten out of her car to talk with me. Her car was facing the opposite direction of my vehicle which meant she had to have come out from the woods. But how could that be? I would have seen the lights on as she came because it was dusk! There was no dirt stirred up on the road from a car driving on it. The car was an old vintage car from the 1960's. It was white with chrome and maroon bucket seats. There was a young adult in the front passenger side, around 15-16 years old, but she never looked up at me. She only looked straight ahead.

My power window didn't work so I had to open my door to her. She told me the Lord told her to stop and pray for me. I immediately thought, *"OK, maybe You* **do** *exist."* I gave her the highlights of my story. She told me she had lost her brother in a painful way and understood the pain I was feeling. She encouraged me to hang on and prayed for me. It wasn't a long exchange but a powerful one.

The next day came and so did hope after a good night's sleep. I had to go to the little country store near my parents and pick up a few things and I ran into her again. I told her how I appreciated her stopping and praying with me and told her thank you for that. She smiled back cordially, said thank you, and wished me a nice day. She turned the corner to go to the next aisle.

I realized I wanted to share with her what I had been thinking in the van before she knocked on my window so I turned around right then and went down the aisle she was on but she wasn't there. I began to look throughout the store in a hurry so I wouldn't miss her. That little country store was only five aisles wide, but there was no sign of her anywhere. I believe with all of my heart that this was an angel encounter. She was sent to encourage me. I was making plans with a lie to separate myself from God at that moment because I couldn't see through the pain of it all.

My friends, God is real. He hears your deepest cries. Trials of all kinds will come, but what I've learned is that they are seasonal. Remember, we "walk *through* the valley of the shadow of death," we don't stay there because "He restores our soul (Psalm 23)."

God sent an angel to help restore my soul during one of the darkest times in my young life. I can name other times He's been there, too. We have to look for Him. He's a God of love and He loves you. Hold on to that fact and trust because He will bring you through. I am living proof of that.

IN CONCLUSION

You know, it doesn't take much to begin something. We usually become engaged with what we start whether it's a project, a book, a game or even dinner. But in the scope of things, beginnings are no small matter. The beginning determines the whole chain of events and even perhaps the outcome.

The Beginning of the Bible

"In the beginning God created…"

Genesis 1:1

I believe these are five of the most important words in the Bible. This is a singular expression of God Himself that He did it all. It all starts with these five words and if we ignore, discount, or even minimize them, well… we do so at our own peril. You see, acknowledging God as our Creator proclaims Him as the ultimate authority over all. He's the Creator of the world, our lives, and our hearts.

When theories try to explain the origins of man through scientific debates what's really happening is that man is beginning his conceited discussion of God's authority. But if we acknowledge that all created beings are under the sovereignty of God then we don't become so self-important anymore. It is a total surrender.

Those who refuse God are a lot like a child who proclaims to his family that he is an orphan. His mother and father are there along with his brothers and sisters; yet the child insists that he does not belong to them, has never seen them before, and has no idea why they all ended up in the same house.

Since he sees himself as an orphan, he has decided his parents have no claim on him. He announces that he will set his own rules. Never mind that he enjoys the warmth of the home, the food in the pantry, and the soft bed and covers in which he sleeps (none of which he labored for either.) This child has torn up his birth certificate and struck out on his own. He can stay up as late as he wants, eat what he wants, and indulge in any or every pleasure he sees fit to.

Note that the child's self-styled freedom has not changed the truths of his origin. All that has changed is his outcome.

He is now *free* to get sick on junk food, become overwhelmed by fatigue, miss family outings, skip the love and embrace of his loved ones—and exclude himself from any inheritance.

This is why our agreement with *"In the beginning God created..."* is so critical. Will we admit and agree we are in the family? Will we agree there is a sovereign authority over us; something much bigger than ourselves.[1]

Without God…

Without God there can be no justice, only the ignorance of the crowd and the whims of the powerful. Without justice there can be no mercy. Without God there can be no holiness and without holiness there is no morality. When morality is nowhere to be found you have no order or safety only acts of personal preference or convenience. Without God there can be no goodness. Without goodness there can be no punishment for evil, only violence and chaos.[2]

We need the redemptive love that Jesus Christ brings. We need to know Him and trust Him with all we do or we will face a never-ending cycle of doubt, fear, and ultimately, misery because we won't be growing. We need the knowledge of how to walk through life when it becomes challenging.

These Books

During the time of writing this book my family and I have been going through some real challenging trials. This study has been immensely helpful for me to walk through and I have leaned hard on the practicality of what James brings. I've used the book of James as a tool box to help my character survive when being tested and challenged.

I have cried like the rest of us when I've been overwhelmed and beaten down by what I'm enduring and what life has thrown at me. But then I've remembered who God is and what He spoke to Job. I've realized how small I am and how big my pride is. I've immediately fallen to my knees with repentance and humility because God is so big and He is sovereign and just. Only then have I been able to surrender it all over to Him.

This has often happened in those intimate, middle of the night times. When I am finally cried out and submit my will to Him, He is tender and loving with me. My circumstances may not have changed, but my countenance has, and so has my relationship with Christ. Things become more personal and then I am able to make another step forward because of Who He is. Day in and day out that's how I survive. I decide to trust that God is bigger and He will help me find my way out.

With Paul's letters to the Thessalonians, I have found hope and strength to continue pressing through. From that I've gained much more wisdom which has brought me hope to endure— at least until the next day. Eventually the crisis passes and I realize I have grown from it. I find it deepened my faith and strengthened my resolve.

Having faith is a matter of not looking at what we see but trusting in the One in whom we do not see.

Another Way to Look at It

Think of yourself as a seed. A sunflower seed is small but no matter where it's planted it grows—reaching and stretching towards the sun standing high and tall.

An acorn seed is small, too. But when it's planted, it grows into a mighty oak tree that can withstand the worst of storms and bring shelter to many who live in its branches. In fact, it actually gains its strength by enduring the storms.

And also remember the apple seed. It is also small and insignificant at first, but when planted and watered it will flourish into an apple tree that over time will bear much fruit that can feed many for years to come.

When all three of these seeds are at the beginning of their life cycle they are little, vulnerable, and unrecognizable to anyone except their Owner who takes the time to plant them.

It's the same way with you and your faith.

We grow and stretch to reach and turn toward the face of the "Son" just like the sunflower does. We can then live lives as mature Christians like James taught us to be.

We withstand the storms of life like the mighty oak does as we dwell on the life of Job. We develop our strengths going through those storms and become a place of refuge and safety for others because of the wisdom and knowledge gained through knowing God's character.

And by following Paul's teachings in his two letters to the Thessalonians, we will be like a well watered and nourished tree bearing much fruit from God's Word for generations to come.

We tend to just look at ourselves as the seed and that's all. But your Creator sees you as the final product not the seed. As we continue to grow in the knowledge of His Word—the good, good soil—we develop, grow and flourish.

But the seed cannot take root unless we really believe in those first five words. Do we *really* believe He created it all? That we are *really* a part of His plan? Do we *really* trust Him with our life regardless of what we may be going through right now?

The answer lies with us. If life is stretching and challenging you right now, ponder these questions and then surrender them to the One who can handle it all—because He can. We just have to trust.

May God abundantly bless you for your desire to grow more in Him. My prayer is for the points made in this study, with the Holy Spirit's help, take root in your heart, and may you bloom where you are planted.

> *"And now, GOD, do it again – bring rains to our drought-stricken lives.*
> *So those who planted their crops in despair, will shout hurrahs at the harvest.*
> *So those who went off with heavy hearts, will come home laughing, with armloads of blessing.*
>
> Psalm 126:4-6 (MSG)

The Creator thinks enough of you to have sent Someone
very special so that you might have life—
abundantly, joyfully, completely and victoriously.
~Anonymous

STUDY QUESTIONS

I'm glad to know you enjoy God's Word and wish to use these questions to dig deeper into what He has for you. My goal with these questions is to provide a way for you to gain even greater knowledge and appreciation for the details and themes found in the books of James, Job, and 1 & 2 Thessalonians.

Here's how to use this guide:
1. You can use the questions for yourself or to lead an open discussion in a group.
2. Use a separate piece of paper to write out your answers.
3. All facts, dates, and information answers can be found in each designated chapter.
4. Please prayerfully consider all your answers, especially those concerning experiences, thoughts, and perspectives.
5. Take your time. Be prayerful about any and all things that the Lord may reveal to you personally.
6. Enjoy the experience of exploring and growing in God's Word.

May the Lord bless your time!

Jill

THE BOOK OF JAMES
GROWING IN MATURITY

Questions from James Introduction: The Challenges

1. How do you see yourself at church and in your community? Are you a giver or a taker?
2. Do you think like a servant leader or just a volunteer?
3. In your own words, write down the difference in the two.
4. Are your eyes focused more on pleasing yourself than on pleasing God? Be honest.
5. How would you evaluate your experience in your prayer life?

Remember;

Prayers are a good indication of our faith. Faith is a gift from God, so ask Him to increase your faith.

Questions from James Chapter 1: Our Faith and Our Trials

1. How does the bible say believers receive wisdom?
2. How does Godly wisdom differ from worldly wisdom?
3. If the trials of life are categorized three ways as Outward trials, Trials from within, and Trials from the Word; personalize this as to what are they in your life?

- What are your Outward trials?
- What are your Trials from within?
- What does God say in His Word that is challenging for you?
- Do you find you are you doubting God? Is this causing double-mindedness? Write down your feelings about it.

4. Do you believe that God cares enough for you to get involved with the intimate details of your life? Do you believe God is good? Is He a gracious, merciful, and faithful God? Think on His character and then make your requests known to Him. Make a list of the attributes that you see in God.
5. James tells us in 1:19 to be "quick to listen, slow to speak and slow to anger." With that said, on a scale of 1-10, how well do you listen and why is it important to be a good listener?
6. In your own words, explain how a person who only hears the Word indulges in self-deception?
7. Describe how a doer of the Word treats the Word and what is the result?
8. How is your spiritual hearing? What is the last thing God has said to you? Are you acting upon it?

Remember;

Just like Joseph, God sees where you're headed—so trust in His leading and not in your circumstances.

Questions from James Chapter 2: Playing Favorites

1. What are the two things that James dealt with in his day that are still prevalent today?
2. What does James want us to show instead?
3. T or F—Did the wealthy ignore the pleas of the poor? Why?
4. Regarding the parable of the unmerciful servant (Matthew 18:21-35), would you agree we act that same way towards our King and Redeemer? Take a moment to write down your offenses (small or big) and ask for God's forgiveness.
5. From Chapter 2, who were the two examples in the Old Testament who put faith into action? Why are they the example?

Remember;

"Do not seek revenge, or bear a grudge against one of your people, but love your neighbor as yourself. I am the Lord."

Leviticus 19:18

Questions from James Chapter 3: There's Power in the Tongue

1. Why do you think James tells us that teachers are judged harder than believers?
2. Proverbs 18:21 says that "The tongue has the power of life and death." Finish Proverbs 12:18 "The words of the reckless _____. Are you watching what you say?
3. What three examples are given to explain how the tongue can control us?
4. According to James 3:6, what does our tongue have the ability to do?
5. Where does earthly wisdom come from?
6. What is heavenly wisdom free of?
7. Fill in the blank; "For the _____ speaks what the _____ is full of." Matthew 12:34

Remember;

"Do not let any unwholesome talk come out of your mouths, but only what is helpful for building others up according to their needs, that it may benefit those who listen."

Ephesians 4:29

Questions from James Chapter 4: Finding Humility

1. Fill in the blank. "Finding humility is not weakness but _____."
2. When we possess hostility toward other believers, can the unbelieving world tell you're a follower of Christ? Give an example of this. If there is resentment toward someone, write their names down and one by one give them to God and ask God to help you not carry the hostility toward them. Don't give those feelings power over you. Surrender it

to God. List their names now and pray with humility to your Creator.
3. "Blessed are the _____, for they will be called _____ __ _____." Matthew 5:9
4. Why should we not compare ourselves to others?
5. Where does our focus go when we take our eyes off of Jesus?
6. What does God have to say about looking at the world? (See Exodus 20:3)

Remember;

Whatever our problems are, our solution is found in humbly submitting ourselves to God as we seek His guidance.

Questions from James Chapter 5: Attitude Adjustments

1. If we are fortunate enough to have wealth, what should our attitude toward the people who work for us be?
2. Where are you storing your treasures these days? Is it here on earth or in heavenly things? Explain.
3. It's ok to enjoy the pleasures of life, but is your faith in them? Are you putting too much of your faith in your worldly pleasures? If there is an example, explain. Remember, the scriptures tell us; *"We brought nothing into the world, and we can take nothing out of it."* (1 Timothy 6:7)
4. How are you doing waiting on God for your prayers to be answered? Are you surrendering to His will for it? Give an example of what you are challenged with in the area of patience.
5. How is your speech? Are you watching not only the language that comes out of your mouth but also the content?
6. "Temptation and testing are two sides of the same coin." Give an example of how you acted with integrity—or didn't. What did you learn from this?
7. Explain how your prayer life is one of thankfulness.

Remember;

"Be joyful always; continually give thanks in all circumstances, for this is God's will for you in Christ Jesus."

1 Thessalonians 5:16-18

THE BOOK OF JOB

THE EXAMPLE

Questions from Job Introduction: The Challenges

1. Even though we don't know the identity of the author of the book of Job, scholars believe it to have been an Israelite. What frequent word was used to describe God in this book that helps prove this point?
2. What makes the Book of Job a unique, one-of-a-kind? Who speaks for four chapters and who speaks for two?
3. When we think of the integrity, wealth, and spiritual sensitivity of Job—with all of the trials he endured, do you think God was acting unjustly? Explain.
4. When God said in Job 1:1 that he [Job] was blameless and upright, did this then mean Job was sinless as well? Explain your answer.

Questions from Job Chapter 1: The Tests and Trials of Job

1. Do you think God was surprised to see Satan enter the courtroom of heaven? Why or why not?
2. Why does Satan challenge Job's motive for worshipping God?
3. In reading Job 1:13-22, what happens to Job?
4. How does Job respond and prove God as good?
5. What does the fact that God sets limits on Satan (see Job 1:12, 2:6) say about Satan's power?

6. What does Job's wife say to him and how does he respond? (Job 2:9-10)
7. Have you ever felt like Job and had loved ones say things like that to you? Explain.
8. What can we learn from this conversation between Job and his wife that will help us relate with friends or loves ones who are suffering?
9. Are you surrounding yourself in an encouraging and friendly environment that won't judge you when trials come upon you? If not, pray the Lord lead you into a place where there is more healthy people who will lift you up and pray with you when you get discouraged.

Remember;

"Let no corrupting talk come out of your mouths, but only such as is good for building up, as fits the occasion, that it may give grace to those who hear."
Ephesians 4:29

Questions from Job Chapter 2: Accusations and Bad Advice

1. Who were Job's three friends who came when they heard he was in distress? _____, _____, and _____.
2. Read Job 4:1-9, 5:17-18. According to Eliphaz why do people suffer?
3. Read Job 8: 1-8. How does Bildad view Job's situation? In your own words, what is his perspective?
4. What attributes of God are missing from Bildad's view of God? Does he see God as a loving God? Do you? (See Lamentations 3:22-33; 1 Timothy 1:13-16)
5. Read Job 11:1-6; 11:13-20. When Zophar speaks, what points does he make?
6. Would you judge a friend who was going through a trial you did not understand? Be honest.
7. What have you learned about the type of friend you are to others? What about the types of friends you have? Are they trustworthy to have with you during difficult times?
8. T / F—"Discouragement is the emotional state of being deprived of hope."

9. What name does Job use for God in Job 19:25-27?
10. Job asks an insightful question in his brief response to Bildad in Job 26:4. How would you answer this question? (See John 8:44).

Remember;

"keeping a clear conscience, so that those who speak maliciously against your good behavior in Christ may be ashamed of their slander."
                                                                    1 Peter 3:16

Questions from Job Chapter 3: Wisdom Comes In All Ages

1. In Chapters 27-37 Job begins to lament God's unjust treatment of him. He is very discouraged. At the center of a discouraged heart they say lies an ungrateful spirit. Would you agree with that statement? Why or why not? Explain.
2. Coming out of discouragement is hard but not impossible. What does God promise in Psalm 55:22? "Cast your cares on _____ _____ and He will sustain you; He will _____ let the righteous be shaken."
3. Who is the fourth friend to come around?
4. Is he a good friend to Job?
5. Elihu mentions in 33:13-19, three ways God speaks to people. What are they?
6. Which of these have you experienced? Explain.
7. Job's perspective was changing due to his sufferings and the bad advice he was getting from his friends. He was losing perspective and believing his own wisdom rather than leaning on God's wisdom. What evidence do we have that God is with us in times of adversity even though we may not be able to "feel" Him with us? (See Deuteronomy 31:6; Romans 8:35-39 for help).
8. How is God helping you to grow more in Him?

Remember;

"You will seek Me and find Me when you seek Me with all your heart."
                                                                    Jeremiah 29:13

Questions from Job Chapter 4: When God Speaks…

1. What is asked for in 31:35 that is granted in 38:1?
2. How does Job 38:36 challenge the view that science, by its very nature, conflicts with the theology of the Bible?
3. How would you relate the implications of God's questions in these verses to Jesus' teaching in Matthew 6:25-33? Explain.
4. Have you ever felt that God was treating you unfairly? What is the right perspective on God regardless of your circumstances?
5. What is your posture when approaching the throne of God? Do you find a place of humility when speaking with Him? Or are you too casual with the Almighty?

Remember,

"We must yield our lives to the supremacy of God. How could we ever be impressed with our "greatness" after beholding God's true grandeur? The only proper response to God's infinite majesty is to bow before Him in total humility, giving Him priority over our lives."

~Stephen J. Lawson

Questions from Job Chapter 5: God Forgives and God Restores

1. In Job 40:1-4, what did Job confess?
2. What brought him to this conclusion?
3. In reality, what had Job been doing when he accused God of being unfair?
4. What conclusion about God does Job voice in Job 42:3? What made him come to this conclusion?
5. How has Job's attitude toward God been changed by this personal encounter?
6. In Job 42:7, why is God angry with Job's friends?
7. Are you doing a good job of accurately representing God to the world around you?
8. Continuing on in Chapter 42, what does God require Job's friends to do to be reconciled to Him and to restore the friendship with

Job? Explain.
9. Did God restore what had been lost? "The LORD _____ the _____ part of Job's life more than the former part." (Job 42:12)
10. If you are going through stressful circumstances or know someone who is;
    - Are you relying on God's truths? Y / N
    - Do you see Him as Sovereign? Y / N
    - Do you possess humility and thankfulness? Y / N
    - What else are you doing? Explain.

Remember;

"Not that we are competent in ourselves to claim anything for ourselves, but our competence comes from God."

2 Corinthians 3:5

THE BOOKS OF 1 & 2 THESSALONIANS

ACTION STEPS

Questions from 1 & 2 Thessalonians: Paul's Challenges

1. Have you ever felt persecuted by someone? Was it a brother or a sister in Christ? Explain.
2. Since Paul teaches about encouragement, what encouragement would you give to people who are being persecuted and oppressed?
3. Who did Paul send to deliver the messages to the church of Thessalonica?
4. If we are taught to demonstrate Christ in our walk, how is your response to impatience and injustice? What about on social media? Are you one way in person and another online?
5. Do your actions line up with what your mouth is speaking or what your fingers are replying to on social media? Give Examples.
6. Is Christ glorified in all you do? Are there areas that need work? Write out what they are and explain (with the Lord's help) how you're going to change and work in this area.

Remember;

"If anyone speaks, they should do so as one who speaks the very words of God. If anyone serves, they should do so with the strength God provides, so that in all things God may be praised through Jesus Christ."

1 Peter 4:11

Questions from 1 & 2 Thess. Chapter 1: Following Paul's Model of Faith

1. What are the reasons Paul thanks God for the Thessalonians? (See 1Thessalonians 1:3)
2. Why is it important that we remember our work, labor, and have endurance?
3. How does 1Thessalonians 1:6 challenge your behaviors or thoughts?
4. Read 1 Thessalonians 1:4-10. What are the signs of true conversions?
5. In Chapter 2, verses 6-9, what qualities do you see in Paul that you appreciate?
6. How can you see these attributes as effective?
7. Paul suggests two different ways of responding to God's Word in 1 Thess. 2:13-14. What are they and how might they relate to you?
8. Having a Christian faith goes far beyond our head knowledge of having a Christian truth. It involves a decision coupled with an action—like walking by faith and not by sight (2 Corinthians 5:7). This takes making a decision from a place of trust and walking that out. Do you believe that God is big enough to help you in that walk of faith with what you're going through? If yes, write out a proclamation to the Lord regarding your challenges. If no, write out a prayer of help and seek your Pastor for guidance.

Remember;

"For we live by faith, not by sight."

2 Corinthians 5:7

Questions from 1 & 2 Thess. Chapter 2: Persecutions and Pressures

1. 2 Timothy 3:12 says, "Everyone who wants to live a godly life in Christ Jesus will be persecuted." Do you think you can stand in the face of opposition? If you have already experienced this at one time—explain. What did you learn?
2. What does Paul fear happened to the young church of Thessalonica? (See 1 Thessalonians. 3:4-10)
3. What brought Paul comfort? (See 1 Thess. 3:6-7)

4. Paul prays for the Thessalonians in 3:11-13. Are you surprised that Paul does not pray for persecution to cease? Why or why not?
5. According to 1 Thess. 4:1-8, what does a life pleasing to God look like?
6. Do you love your spiritual family and long to spend quality time with them? Or is Christian fellowship on the fringes of your life? (Read John 13:35 before you answer)

Remember;

A pearl becomes a gem and valuable only through the agitation it has to go through.

Questions from 1 & 2 Thess. Chapter 3: Living a Life of Readiness

1. What is your view of God in view of death?
2. What is the hope that allows Christians to grieve differently than those without hope?
3. What are the truths recorded in 1 Thess. 4:16-17?
4. In 1 Thess. 4:18, what command is given after "therefore?"
5. How would those things encourage you if you were grieving over a loss of a loved one?
6. When Paul speaks of The Day of the Lord, what does he mean? (See 1 Thess. 5:1-4)
7. Read 2 Peter 3:10-18. How does this add to your understanding of this day? What else did you learn?
8. How does Paul reassure the Thessalonians concerning their future in 1 Thess. 5:9-11?
9. Do you have assurance? How would you reassure someone in doubt?
10. Name some ways you can be an encouragement to someone who is concerned about life after death?

Remember,

"Now faith is confidence in what we hope for and assurance about what we do not see."

Hebrews 11:1

Questions from 1 & 2 Thess. Chapter 4: Justice, Encouragement & Warning

1. What commands does Paul give in 1 Thess. 5:13-15?
2. Which of these commands do you find most challenging? Explain.
3. How could you incorporate them into your life?
4. Paul says to be joyful always. Do you believe he meant that literally? Why or why not?
5. Read 2 Thessalonians 1:1-10. In verse 6, what does Paul say will happen "when the Lord Jesus is revealed from heaven?"
6. What would you say to someone who struggles with a God who inflicts punishments on others for doing wrong?
7. How would knowing these things help the persecuted Thessalonians not want to get revenge for the hurt that they are feeling? (See Romans 12: 12-20)
8. Throughout these letters Paul is praying for the Thessalonians. In 2 Thess. 1:11-12, what is his prayer from these verses?
9. How might the name of Jesus be glorified in you?

"Yesterday I was clever, so I took the glory for me. Today He makes me wise, so I give the glory to Thee"

~Indonesia123

Questions from 1 & 2 Thess. Chapter 5: Standing in Truth

1. What has caused the Thessalonians to become alarmed in 2 Thessalonians 2:2-3?
2. What is the nature of their concerns and their confusion?
3. In 2 Thess. 2:3, what perspective does Paul offer?
4. According to 2 Thess. 2:10-12, why is loving the truth so important?
5. Do you think there is a difference between believing the truth and loving the truth? Explain.
6. Paul speaks a blessing over the Thessalonians in 2:16-17. What aspect of this blessing would you like to pray for yourself? What would you say about someone else? with, What aspect of this blessing would you like to pray for yourself and for others?

7. Can you think of a specific situation in which you would like the Lord to bless you?

If Timothy came to visit you and reported back to Paul, what evidence in your life would he see that would give him "confidence in the Lord" about you? What strengths are you possessing?

As I said in the Conclusion—we see ourselves as only the vulnerable seed, but God sees the final product that seed will become. Trust in God's leading and not in your circumstances. Surrender to His timing for your life and dwell on His love for you because He loves you so deeply and wants the best for you.

What are the three main things you want to remember about God from this study? Explain.

Endnotes:

The Book of James
1. Community Bible Study, TD helps, James 2009, Lesson 1, pg. 3
2. Engaging God's Word: James, 2012, pg. 13
3. Community Bible Study TD helps James, 2009; Lesson 2 pg 6
4. Ibid, pg 5
5. Ibid, pg 5
6. Lamentations 3:22-23
7. http://Biblehub.com/greek/4382.htm
8. Community Bible Study, TD helps- James 2009, Lesson 3, pg 9
9. Ibid, pg 9
10. Thomas D. Lea, James- Holman New Testament Commentary 1999, B & H Publishing Group, Nashville, TN, pg 303
11. Community Bible Study, TD helps James, 2009, Lesson 4, pg 12
12. Ibid, pg 12
13. Community Bible Study, TD helps, James lesson 5, 2009, pg 14
14. Thomas D. Lea, James- Holman New Testament Commentary 1999, B & H Publishing Group, Nashville, TN, pg 318
15. Community Bible Study, TD helps, James lesson 5, 2009, pg 15
16. Ibid, pg 16
17. Thomas D. Lea, James- Holman New Testament Commentary 1999, B & H Publishing Group, Nashville, TN, pg 341
18. Hetty Green; mentalfloss.com/article/49379/life-and-times-hetty-hoarder-witch-wall-street
19. Luci Swindoll; NIV Women's Devotional New Testament with Psalms and Proverbs, 1990, 1993 by Zondervan Publishing House
20. Community Bible Study, TD helps, James lesson 6 2009, pg 18
21. Ibid, pg 18

The Book of Job
1. Community Bible Study, TD helps Job, 2010, Lesson 1, pg 2
2. Ibid, pg 2
3. Keith Meyering, Discipleship Journal, issue #49, pg 41
4. David Wallechinsky, The Complete Book of the Olympics, Readers Digest

5. NIV Study Bible, copyright 1985, Zondervan Corperation, Introduction to Job, pg 732.
6. Community Bible Study TD helps, Job, 2010 Lesson 2, pg 6
7. Stephen J. Lawson, Job- Holman Old Testament Commentary, 2004, B & H Publishing Group, pg. 33
8. Ibid, pg 51
9. Ibid, pg 9
10. Ibid, pg 59
11. Community Bible Study, TD helps, Job Lesson 4- pg. 11
12. Ibid, pg 11
13. Stephen J. Lawson, Holman Old Testament Commentary, 2004 B & H Publishing Group, pg 237-38
14. Ibid, pg 9
15. Ibid, pg 284
16. Ibid, pg 294
17. https://en.wikipedia.org/wiki/Zeus
18. Stephen J. Lawson, Holman Old Testament Commentary, 2004 B & H Publishing Group, pg. 307
19. Ibid, pg 322
20. Ibid, pg 313
21. Stephen J. Lawson, Holman Old Testament Commentary, 2004 B & H Publishing Group, Pg. 325-26
22. http://www.Biblestudytools.com/dictionaries/bakers-evangelical-dictionary/know-knowledge.html
23. Stephen J. Lawson, Holman Old Testament Commentary, 2004 B & H Publishing Group, pg. 333
24. Jill Grossman, A Revelation of Love; A Comprehensive Study Companion to the Book of Revelation, 2015 WordCrafts Press, pg 103
25. Community Bible Study, TD helps 2009, Job Lesson 6 pg 17
26. Ibid, pg. 17

The Books of 1 & 2 Thessalonians
1. Community Bible Study, TD helps, 2009, 1 Thessalonians Lesson 1, pg 2
2. Ibid, pg 2
3. Engaging God's Word: 1 and 2 Thessalonians, 2013, Community

Bible Study, pg 13
4. Knute Larson, Holman New Testament Commentary, 2000, B & H Publishing Group, pg 22
5. Ibid, pg 22
6. Ibid, pg 22
7. Ibid, pg 23
8. Ibid, pg 19
9. Knute Larson, Holman New Testament Commentary, 2000 B & H Publishing Group, pg 44
10. Stream in the Desert, 1997, Zondervan Publishing House, pg 188
11. 1992 by Oswald Chambers Publications Association, Ltd. Original edition, 1935, Dodd, Mead, & Company, Inc. – July 4th
12. Ibid, pg 31
13. Ibid, pg 32
14. Ibid, pg 39
15. Community Bible Study, TD helps, 1 & 2 Thess. Lesson 4, pg 11
16. Ibid, pg 11
17. Knute Larson, Holman New Testament Commentary, 2000 B & H Publishing Group, pg 97
18. Turn Your Eyes Upon Jesus, by Helen H. Lemmel, Public Domain
19. https://en.wikipedia.org/wiki/Caligula
20. http://penelope.uchicago.edu/~grout/encyclopaedia_romana/gladiators/nero.html
21. Community Bible Study, TD helps 2009, 2 Thess. Lesson 6, pg. 17
22. Ibid, pg 17
23. Knute Larson, Holman New Testament Commentary, 2000 B & H Publishing pg 87
24. Ibid, pg 87-88
25. http://churchleaders.com/pastors/pastor-articles/167067-jen-hatmaker-conference-uninvited-me-to-speak.html/3
26. Community Bible Study, TD helps 2009, 2 Thess. Lesson 6, pg 18

In Conclusion
1. Knute Larson, Holman New Testament Commentary, 2000 B & H Publishing, pg. 115
2. Ibid, pg 115

ACKNOWLEDGEMENTS

I love learning about God's Word and the Good News of the Gospel which brings me into a deeper relationship with Him. With that said, I would first like to thank my Lord, Jesus Christ, for always wooing me closer to Him with His Word. I never want to stop growing and learning!

I also want to thank my loving husband, Steve. What would I do without you? You have held my hand throughout this process with encouragement and edits! You and I have been through lots of "life," but I can't imagine going through any of it without you, honey. I'd also like to thank my kids, Kayce and Jennah. Your wisdom and input helps me more than you could ever know. I'm very proud of both of you and I love the way you choose to love your heavenly Father. May God continue to bless you and give you favor.

A heartfelt thank you to Mike and Paula Parker at Wordcrafts Press for being in my corner and helping me grow as a writer. Also to the talented David Warren for lending your creativity of imagery to my books and for always making me look good in the photos you take too! Thank you, David, you're the best! A special thanks to Keith Cohl at Soundmark Productions for all of your help on the audio version of this book and to Jonathan Grisham for adding the music.

I would also like to thank my close girlfriends who walk through the thick and thin of life with me. Joy, Ann, Karen, Cindi, and Donna—you guys have been there for me in so many ways and I am forever grateful to have you in my corner.

ABOUT THE AUTHOR

Jill Grossman is an author, teacher and speaker based in Nashville, Tennessee. She and her husband Steve, own and operate Erchomai Counseling and Coaching. Erchomai (pronounced *er-ko-my*) is a Greek word that means "Come, be established" and she and her husband help individuals and couples become established in identity, purpose and God's Word.

Jill has taught several bible studies and has podcasts available for your convenience. You can visit her website, jillgrossman.com, or go to her Facebook page too.

Jill's been married for 31 years and has two adult children, Kayce and Jennah. Jill is an ordained pastor and is currently working toward her Master's degree in Christian counseling. She enjoys singing around town with her jazz trio and acting in local theater productions as well. But her true joy comes from teaching and speaking.

She understands that to find your purpose and identity in life, the answers are found in knowing and understanding God's character through God's Word.

Jill and her husband attend Peytonsville Church in Thompson Station, Tennessee, where they are under the covering and teaching of Pastor Larry Randolph.

Jill is available to come and speak at your church or conference and you can contact her at jillgrossman.com. You can connect with Jill further by "liking" her on Facebook, too.

Also Available From

Jill Grossman

A Revelation of Love
A Comprehensive Study Companion to the Book of Revelation

Also Available From

WordCrafts Press

Pro-Verb Ponderings
31 Ruminations on Positive Action
by Rodney Boyd

Morning Mist
Stories from the Water's Edge
by Barbie Loflin

Why I Failed in the Music Business
and how NOT to follow in my footsteps
by Steve Grossman

Youth Ministry is Easy!
and 9 other lies
by Aaron Shaver

Chronicles of a Believer
by Don McCain

Illuminations
by Paula K. Parker & Tracy Sugg

A Scarlet Cord of Hope
by Sheryl Griffin

www.wordcrafts.net

www.ingramcontent.com/pod-product-compliance
Lightning Source LLC
Chambersburg PA
CBHW070604300426
44113CB00010B/1403